THE
QUIET
HOUSE

The Quiet House
Reflections on the Loss of a Spouse

The Quiet House
978-1-7910-2880-0
978-1-7910-2881-7 eBook

Also by Ronald J. Greer:

The Path of Compassion:
Living with Heart, Soul, and Mind

Now That They Are Grown:
Successfully Parenting Your Adult Children

Markings on the Windowsill:
A Book About Grief That's Really About Hope

If You Know Who You Are, You Will Know What to Do:
Living with Integrity

THE
QUIET
HOUSE

Reflections on the Loss of a Spouse

RONALD J. GREER

Abingdon Press | Nashville

The Quiet House
Reflections on the Loss of a Spouse

Library of Congress Control Number: 2023935970
978-1-7910-2880-0

MANUFACTURED IN THE
UNITED STATES OF AMERICA

To Karen,

whose spirit, wisdom, and inspiration

will always go with me.

Contents

"My story is important not because it is mine, God knows, but because if I tell it anything like right, the chances are you will recognize that in many ways it is also yours."

—Frederick Buechner

Preface

It was Thanksgiving Day, about four o'clock in the afternoon. I had not known how the day would go. None of us did. It was our family's first holiday since my wife Karen's death less than three months before. Her engaging personality and caring spirit had been at the center of each of these occasions. So, as we gathered, we each took a deep breath and braced ourselves for the plunge into unknown waters.

I have a family who loves and enjoys each other, as we did again on that Thanksgiving. The day together went as well as it possibly could. Prior to the meal I had taken a moment to read from my journaling of that morning—to acknowledge how we had been blessed for all the years with Karen's presence and were now blessed with the memories and her spirit living within us and among us.

It was a good day. We ate well, savored each other's company, and remembered Karen. This occasion was tender, to be sure, but one filled with the usual bursts of laughter.

Soon it was late afternoon. The day had gone by so quickly. Now it was time for my children and the grands to pack up and drive back to their homes. We hugged goodbye. I waved as they pulled down the driveway, staying to watch them until they were completely out of sight. I then slowly turned and walked back to the house. I took a deep breath as I opened the door and stepped into the hallway.

The house had never felt so empty. The tears came before I got to the end of the hall and continued through the afternoon. The raw sadness of walking back into our house alone was nearly unbearable. It felt like Karen had died all over again. I had never been without her on any holiday for half a century. I had never waved goodbye to our kids and walked back in without my life partner. Never. Never had I felt so alone. Never had I felt such silence, such stillness.

The house was so quiet.

A Ray of God's Light

I have written of grief before. It was my first book, written years ago following the death of our young son. In this writing I want to feel free in exploring grief and mourning, so I will not be concerned if I have covered an issue before. If the matter is important, I will take the topic from the top, looking at it again from my perspective today. I will simply tell my story and share my reflections on it.

This is not a textbook or a clinical description of grief. You will find those elsewhere. These are reflections by a married partner who lost his spouse of almost fifty years. I am also a pastoral counselor who has walked similar paths with counseling clients for decades. This book is primarily for those who have lost a husband or a wife—or those who want to learn more about that grief. The death of a spouse is a different loss. I have said goodbye to a child, to my parents, to dear friends, and now to my wife. Each is unique, and I want to share from my experience, personally and professionally, something of the path that may lie ahead.

This writing is not really about death and dying so much as it is about life and living on. As I put it in that earlier writing, this book is on grief, but it's really about hope.

As a pastoral counselor, I will be using images from my faith. I am not pushing that faith onto you. I am tapping into its rich heritage to illustrate universal truths, just as I trust Rabbi Harold Kushner would draw from his Jewish background or the Dalai Lama from his Buddhist legacy. I write from the only background I have. As I use images of my faith, let them remind you of the parallel images from yours. Both point to the truth.

There will be themes in this writing to which I will circle back, as I return to them to highlight their importance in different contexts.

I will tell you my story—my life with Karen and my grief without her. But, as I do, know that my story is not the point. I tell it to remind you of your story. And your loss. Place mine beside yours to see how it resonates with your experience. See if it reveals any new insight from where you have been, enabling you to see your story with a new clarity and a richer meaning. Perhaps the experiences of our journeys will be similar, and you will nod in agreement as you read. Or you may find new clarity as you are reminded of meaningful moments in which your path took a different and distinctive turn from mine. And, either way, as we reflect together, we may not feel quite so alone on the journey.

I had known Karen for fifty years, married for forty-nine of them. I wish each of you reading this had known her, as I would have been enriched to have known your loved one. She was a joy, as was our life together. I have countless memories of that life, but the one that most readily comes to mind happened—of all places—in our garage.

I was leaving one morning for the office. She was struggling with cancer and its treatments, fatigued much of the time. She awakened early that morning and came downstairs. She found her comfortable place on the sofa and tucked herself under her blanket. We chatted for a moment. Then I made her cup of tea, kissed her goodbye, and headed for the car.

As I opened the car door to get in, to my surprise, the door from the house to the garage opened. Karen was tired, but there she stood, looking at me with the broadest smile. "Ron," she said, "go be a ray of God's light."

A ray of God's light. That is what I hope to bring in this writing.

Why I Mourn

I have cautioned others for years about the importance of not idealizing their loved ones who die. Doing so airbrushes out the negative and sees them as saints. It's like the husband who once said, "There are two perfect men who have ever lived. Jesus Christ and my wife's first husband who died." Idealizing distorts the memory. It does not lead to healthy mourning because it is not grieving the whole person, the real person who died—only an ideal dimension of them.

My thoughts on Karen are not magnified because she died. How I see her today is how I have always seen her. In fact, the dedication page of my first book in 2006 begins, "To Karen, from whom I have learned of courage, hope, and grace."

She always chose joy.

Karen was no Pollyanna. She didn't imagine the positive. Instead, she looked for what was authentically positive about her life and her world. After a week in the hospital, only days before she died, Karen's physician called me. She was struggling with focus, and he wanted to be sure we understood what was medically important. The next day, following a good night's rest back at home, Karen and I talked. I quoted his words to her. He said unless certain things began changing, then "this could be the beginning of the end." She paused for a moment. Then she looked at me and said, "Well, if it is, it's been a wonderful life."

This was not denial. Reality, especially in those final days, was abundantly clear. No, it was choosing to focus on what was true and positive and sacred in life. She believed "the garden you water is the garden you grow."

She looked at her world with wonder and awe. When the grandchildren came over, she would take them to the backyard and have them look for the prettiest thing they could find. They each then came back with their reports.

The person Karen was didn't happen by accident. Every morning when she woke up, after she opened her eyes but before she got out of bed, she prayed. Her prayer was for God to help her be her very best self, to be the Karen God wanted her to be. She lived her life that intentionally. She would go to the clinic for an infusion and everyone with whom she came in contact was infused with the spirit of her loving-kindness.

She was joyful and filled with laughter, but she was substantial and lived with wisdom. Her positive spirit was grounded. It wasn't fluff. Our son Eric died at two years of age in an accident. A month after his death, this grieving mother said to me, "We are going to make it through this and have fun and enjoy ourselves again. Because if we don't, then Eric will not have been the only one who died." Strength of character. Courage of will. Wisdom under fire.

In her final days, Karen and I talked every so often about what we knew was coming. She was far more at peace with her dying than I was. Near the very end, perhaps two weeks before she died, we were in the kitchen talking…about her dying. My sadness overwhelmed me, and I burst into tears. She stepped over to me and wrapped her arms around me. I don't know how long I stood there crying, but however long it was, with those now-frail arms of hers, she quietly and firmly held me.

Finally, I finished. Karen stepped back, and we looked at each other. It was then that the obvious dawned on me. *She* was holding *me* as *I* was crying about *her* dying. As our eyes met, I laughed and said, "Isn't there something backwards about this? Aren't I supposed to be comforting you?" We laughed together. No, she knew her time had come. She was ready "to go home," and I was not ready for her to leave. There was that wisdom and strength in her that accepted this last chapter ending. And what she felt was peace, the peace with which she lived her last days.

I have had several people say to me they will remember her *presence*. One friend wrote referring to her as having "a weight of presence and a lightness of touch." She was present, both because she valued the relationship with the person with whom she was talking and because she believed in living in the present moment.

This is how she expressed it in words she spoke to our Sunday school class, "Each day is the most important one that we have, and we should live it so that at its end we have nothing to regret, no 'Thank you,' 'I love you,' or 'I'm sorry' left unsaid. No teaching or learning left undone."

Karen would say increasingly toward the end of her life, "Don't look back." Of course, she loved looking back at the memories, but what she meant was to live in the moment. Show up. Be present. She was aware that her days were increasingly limited, and she didn't want to waste a single one of them. She wanted us to savor every moment, to be fully alive.

This is the lady with whom my life was blessed. This is the lady I lost. So, you understand why I mourn.

Darkness

You turn these pages with courage. As you open the windows to your soul, you acknowledge the reality of our shared darkness. You are here to be real. It is a vulnerable thing to do, to open yourself to how you feel—the emptiness, the loss, the heartache, the grief, even the despair.

We know heartache. Too well. We have lost those who were as dear to us as life itself. We have looked straight into the face of grief. We have seen the darkening clouds gather over us.

Perhaps it was as the oncologist, with his gaze to the floor, said, "It doesn't look good." Or perhaps when we walked with our spouse out of the neurologist's office haunted by the prognosis we had heard. Or when we agreed it was time to call hospice, or, later, as we visited the cemetery.

Or maybe it was when, out of the blue, a new acquaintance asked the innocent question, "And are you married?" and we struggled not to sob.

We know the darkness.

We know it well. At times, pitch black. The darkness that settled over many of our worlds was incredible. We stood over their graves at first in disbelief, then despair, in unspeakable pain at how life could go on without them. We know the darkness.

But we do not sit passively in the dark. We look for at least flickers of light—the light that gives us hope. We look for ways to navigate through—and, hopefully, one day, beyond—this darkened landscape.

We look for hope. But it must be real hope. The lights of hope must be substantial, grounded, and true. Not those silly cliches we heard at the funeral home, thank you very much. We need something real. It is the truth that sets us free.

Hope is not fantasy. Hope, as I use the term, is never wishful thinking. Hope is a positive expectation grounded in reality. It is to expect with confidence. With that in mind, we look for hope. We look for those flickers of light.

Yet, we are not naive. We don't expect too much of the light just now. Not yet. We were never promised the brilliance of daylight on this path, but we do long for light in our darkness, hope in our despair, direction in our mourning, and support in our loneliness.

And I find there is light—not enough to *eliminate* the darkness but enough to *illuminate* our way through it. Yes, illumination is what we are seeking. The light illuminating our path, if only a few steps ahead, showing us where we are to go, how we are to travel this steep, winding, and rocky trail.

And you have sought a Sherpa as your guide. A fellow pilgrim. You have invited me, each of us with lantern in hand, to be that Sherpa with you on this leg of your journey. As it has been said, I am not the "sage on the stage" but the "guide by your side." We walk together.

The Work of Grief

I have had several friends, with heart-felt compassion, say to me, "I wish I could take away your pain." My response has been, "If you could, I would ask that you didn't." I need my pain, my grief to work this through. I need to mourn, and the pain of my grief pushes me to let the tears flow. Without my grief I would have no tears, no means to get through this valley. Mourning is that vehicle that moves me through. Without my grief I would have nothing pulling me to mourn and, ultimately, to heal.

Memorial services are often referred to as Services of Celebration. And, indeed, they are, for these services are in celebration of lives well-lived. But for those who mourn, these are not *times* of celebration. If that phrase on the cover of the program for your spouse's service feels like a contradiction to how you feel, it should. You honor the life of the one you love in celebration; but you honor the heart that beats within you in deep, personal grief.

I have come to respect my grief.

Make no mistake, I detest hurting. And though it is heartbreaking in its pain, grief is one of those healthy, healing emotions. It is in the league with hunger and loneliness. As hunger is the body's discomforting reminder for nutrition, and loneliness is the heart's call for relationship, grief is the soul's urging for continued mourning in order to heal and move forward.

We seek to heal. Our hearts have been broken, and we want to be whole again. The origin of the word *heal* goes back, not surprisingly, with the term *health* to the English word *whole*. To be whole is to be sound, complete. We seek wholeness to our lives, so shattered by our heartbreaking loss. These lives of ours will always be different, the tenderness will go with us because our spouses do not, but we can be whole again. To be whole, to be healthy means to heal, and to heal is to respect our grief.

Grief is the emotional blow that hits us with our loss. Grief is the heartache we feel. Grief is also complex. It begins with sadness, but it also includes loneliness, confusion, emptiness, and the indescribable pain of loss. The word *grief* comes from the Latin "gravis" meaning "heavy." How accurate is *that*? It is no surprise it shares its origin with our word "gravity." When we grieve, we feel the emotional weight of the sorrow, the anguish. It can hit at any time. With no warning. The next wave of grief simply emerges from deep within. And, once again, it is time to mourn.

Let me pause here to make a distinction between the words *grief* and *mourning*. Grief is the painful, emotional reaction to loss. We have no choice in the matter. Life hits us with the sorrow, and we double over in pain. That's grief.

Mourning is giving a voice to that pain. Mourning is intentionally letting it out. Mourning is openly expressing our grief.

Grief is not optional. Mourning is—and it is wise to opt for it. Grief is felt intuitively with the loss. Mourning is intentionally choosing to engage and express pain. Grief involves saying goodbye. Mourning, then, involves tears. Lots and lots of tears.

Mourning requires courage. We wisely engage it. We courageously engage it. The life ahead can only be accomplished by looking squarely into that agonizing emotion that comes with every major loss.

"Give it a voice" is the way I have encouraged mourning over the years. Have the courage to feel all that you feel and express it. Give it a voice. Openly. Bring it up from the depth of your heart and let it out.

Cry it out.

Talk it out.

Write it out (for those who journal, and I encourage it).

It has been said, "First you cry. Then you cry some more." Yet tears come in different forms. They may come down our cheeks or in emotions spoken to a precious friend or in words written in a journal in the early morning hours. Each expresses our grief. Each promotes healing of the heart. Each can be vital avenues of our mourning.

Honor your grief in ways that are right for you. Everyone is a unique human being and every marriage is a unique relationship—so you will mourn the loss of your spouse in your own distinctive way. Mourn your loss in ways that have integrity for you. I have honored how I need to do it, which I will share with you. Please honor how your heart calls you to do it.

The love of your life has died. About that, you had no choice. What you will do with the emotions that leaves you is completely in your hands. Choose purposefully and choose wisely.

I want genuinely to work through my grief. I do not want simply to let time pass, distancing myself from Karen's death until it is no longer as vivid or the wound as raw, allowing me to ignore the pain because it has become less focused and severe. Then calluses may have formed so I no longer feel what is beneath them. That's not healing. It's repression, denial—which may later lead to depression. I do not want to close off my heart. Should I deny my grief, I also may—without intent or awareness—ultimately reduce the experience of other emotions, such as joy and happiness. I do not want to begin diminishing my emotional life simply because these feelings are difficult.

If I am to heal, I must actively mourn, not passively hurt.

Hope is found through expression. It is not found in denial. The way we begin to glimpse lights of hope in our grief is not to go around it or try to get over it but courageously to go straight through it. Hope is found in engaging the mourning—actively, openly, passionately. Mourning is a process. Respect it, trust it, be patient with it as you give yourself to it.

27

Coming as a Child

We live in a culture that fears death because it fears the pain of loss that comes with it. I understand the resistance. Grief hurts. But, with my years as a pastoral counselor, I also understand the depression that usually comes with repressed grief. What I encourage—and intentionally live by—is to look as directly as I can stand into the pain, to let the next wave wash over me without distraction or dilution. To mourn from the depth of my heart. To know that my healing one day will come from the decision to grieve on this day.

It was years ago. I shall always remember that afternoon in the chapel of our church. I had been asked to give the prayer at the memorial service of a friend who had died far too young. In that moment of silence, as I stepped to the pulpit to offer the prayer, his six-year-old daughter, seated on the second pew, started to cry. You could hear her begin with a whimper. Then quickly, uncontrollably she began to sob—gasping for breath between each wail.

Wrapped in her mother's arms she continued to let out her pure, raw grief. It still gives me chills as I think of it. The depth of her grief had thrown the windows to her soul wide open—so intense and passionate was her emotion, expressed as openly as only a child could.

No one heard a word of that prayer. Every heart in the chapel went out to this child and was riveted on her pain. It was a profound and sacred moment.

Since that day I have never walked into a funeral service or stood beside a grave or taken a seat in my counseling office with anyone suffering a loss without an empathy more sharply focused from that afternoon. How do I put it? I will forever remember her voice, her pure grief.

We can fake it, to others and even to ourselves. But behind all the defenses and disguises and sophistications adults use to hide, we are the walking wounded . . . in times of grief and mourning, the pure pain of that child's voice is truly each of our voices.

"Unless you come to me as a child," Jesus said, and, indeed, on this journey each of us do.

You and I have taken on some challenges in our lifetimes, but nothing is quite like this one. Mourning is a challenge, and it is one we must not dodge. It must be engaged, if we are to heal and successfully move forward with our lives. No matter how much it hurts as we sob, we remember that it is healthy. It gives us traction in moving through. Let your tears cleanse the wound to promote your healing.

Mourn. Courageously mourn.

Each Loss Is Different

The impact of each loss is defined by the uniqueness of that relationship. Who that person was to you and what that person meant in your life will determine the expanse of your loss, your grief, and your heartache.

I don't compare the emotional impact of losses. Each is different, and each is subjective.

I don't compare the impact, but I do compare the uniqueness of losses. Experiences of grief have distinctive characteristics. Having lost parents, a child, and a life partner, I am aware of the similarities and the differences. Each is profound in its own way and each is qualitatively different from the other.

The death of a parent severs us from our past, the death of a spouse from our present, and the death of a child from our future.

From our earliest awareness, we assume our parents will predecease us. It will be sad. We will feel grief. But, unless the circumstances are especially tragic, it likely will not be traumatic. Make no mistake, the pain will be real, but it will be felt in the natural progression of life as it is designed.

The death of a child, of any age, is distinctly different. Our children are supposed to bury us. We are to care for them, nurture them, rear them into maturity, and let them go. Then, one day, in the natural order of life, we will die, and their lives will continue on. It is not to be the other way around. When that happens, our hearts are broken as we rebel against it, as we mourn the inconceivable. It feels like a contradiction of nature.

The death of a child is the loss of this precious relationship, of our future together, and of their future beyond us, as every parent anticipates and dreams it will be. Plus, with a child, there is often a private feeling of guilt—no matter the circumstances or the cause of death—for we are to protect them and keep them alive.

The death of a spouse truly is more connected with the loss of our present. It differs from the death a child, in that, from the day of the wedding, we always knew one of us would have to say goodbye to the other. It's right there in the vows: "until death do us part." This hardly minimizes the impact of the loss; it simply frames it as one we ultimately knew was coming.

When we lose a spouse, so much of our lives change like the ending of no other relationship. It is different from any other death, and painfully so. Karen's life and mine were so intertwined day in and day out, both emotionally and literally.

"The two shall become one flesh" is how the scriptures describe marriage (Mark 10:8). Implied in the verb tense of "shall become" means, though we will never fully arrive, marriage, at its best, is to be a relationship that is always deepening, connecting, maturing. Ever closer. With the aspiration of becoming so close, so in step, so intimate, we are as one.

Then, as "one," our other half dies. That is how it feels. Not just that we have lost our life partner but that a part of us has died.

Suddenly this beautiful process of uniting is ruptured. We were moving closer and closer . . . and suddenly she is gone.

No! This just can't be!

We were partners in this life. We lived it together. When she and I suffered every other loss, we mourned together. Yet with this loss, I sit here alone. This one is different. It is the loss of that cherished companionship. Yes, the loss of that emotional, personal intimacy of our life companions.

For many of us, as our life partner is slowly dying, we have some of the most precious, intimate moments of our marriage. Their dying may open our awareness as never before, savoring each of those moments with the realization that the window is closing. It is a final blessing. We thank God for these memories we will carry with us forever, though it means we became even closer and the loss even deeper in the final goodbye.

And with the loss of a spouse, unlike any other loss, the reminders are everywhere! Your lives are all wrapped up in each other and there isn't a room or a closet or any corner in the house that doesn't remind you of their life and of their death.

You interacted throughout the day. Countless times something will happen, and I will think to myself, "I've got to tell Karen about that"—only to remember.

With a chuckle in his voice, a friend was telling me of a series of events his wife had planned that he did not wish to attend. He first spoke with levity, and then his expression suddenly changed. His eyes looked to the floor for an extended moment. He looked back up and said, "I bet you're thinking, 'I would give anything to be able to take my wife *anywhere* right now.'"

Yes, I would give anything.

My wife and my son are buried together on a little knoll, side by side. I know their spirits are everywhere, but when I visit their graves, I talk with them there. I just chat. At times, I feel the joy of having their spirits in my life, yet often I feel the profound loss that they are no longer physically here. As I look from one grave to the other, it is a different relationship with which I am connecting. Parent to child. Life partner to life partner. Different relationships and different losses.

So, each is distinct. Now, I deal with the death of my spouse. My partner in life, to whom I had to say goodbye.

There is a little plaque in our kitchen Karen gave me years ago. It reads, "You are my happily ever after." And she was mine. And now she is gone. How will I live happily now? How do I live happily after my "happily ever after" is gone?

That is the loss and that is the question you and I have set out to explore.

33

The Journey Alone

The journey of mourning is a process. A process of healing—toward accepting what is and looking to what is becoming.

I had a great life. Now I have a good one. I must remember that. This was such a huge hit to my heart; I have to be intentional in remembering the quality of the life I still have. I must mourn Karen's death—but not be defined by it. As Alfred Lord Tennyson put it, "Though much is taken, much abides."

It remains a good life. It is filled with a loving family, dear friends, meaningful work, and a strong faith. It is a blessed life. So much is good. Because of the magnitude of my loss, I must not lose perspective of the life I have and on which I will build.

It has been said, "There are some losses you never get over. You learn how best you will live with them." Those are the big ones. The big losses. With them, it is not that there isn't a rich, full life ahead. No, that is within our reach, if we choose for it to be. But for the heartaches most deeply felt, there will always be a special place of tenderness that will remain. They meant too much to us for it to be otherwise.

The journey begins with our being doubled over with raw grief. Later, the grief will morph into the sadness of sorrow.

And, finally, we are left with an ongoing tenderness. This tends to be the broad arc of our mourning: a time of grief, a time of sorrow, and a lifetime of tenderness.

Though those places in our hearts will continue to be felt, we will heal. Wherever you are on your path, know that you can achieve that healthy, purposeful life in spite of your heartache.

So, where is this path to a new meaningful life? It is not steps to be completed but a process to be engaged.

In the journey through this valley, we are always back and forth with our emotions. We never know to which one we might awaken next. It is never linear or undeviating. And to live a full, meaningful life we must deal directly and openly with each emotion as it comes.

Yet, in spite of these spontaneous hearts of ours, there tends to be that progression toward healing and wholeness. A development toward a new life and a new identity.

We are no longer *where* we were. We are no longer *who* we were. And we are not yet where or who we ultimately will be. The ship has left the port, and the destination is yet to be discovered. All we know is that we have engaged the healing process we call mourning, intent on working this through to a new and meaningful life.

The scriptures speak to this. In a Psalm that repeatedly affirms the faithfulness of God, one of its teachings begins with the painful truth, "Weeping may linger for the night." And then the psalmist adds, "but joy comes with the morning" (Psalm 30:5b). In the journey of our grief, the day will break, morning will come. We enter "the darkest valley" knowing it is a valley we will walk *through*, not one in which we will permanently reside (Psalm 23:4a).

My own experience echoes what I have heard from countless others who have made similar journeys. Let me share what we have learned simply as markers or guideposts you may see on your way. I offer them, as it has been said, to be descriptive and not prescriptive. Everyone's path is their own.

Yet, after the early weeks of pure emotional chaos following the loss of a spouse, most enter this space in which they will go through seasons of deep grief and mourning, through ongoing sorrow with signs of healing, through periods of transition, redefining much of their lives, and then, much later, into a new life of purpose and meaning and even joy.

At First

"This can't be. It just can't be."

The grief of the early weeks doesn't come in waves. No, it's a continuous flood—of grief and pain. Our partners' absence is the first thought in the morning and the final awareness as we turn out the lights for the day.

It doesn't matter if the death was sudden or coming at the end of an extended illness—when that moment comes, it just can't be. We are fully aware of the reality before us, but it just can't be. We are not in denial, but we are, for a time, disoriented. Stunned by our new reality. Trying to get our sea legs. Trying desperately to take in what has just happened.

After half a century of waking up with Karen in the morning, of her walking through the door throughout the day, of having dinner together each evening, I came to expect it as a central part of my life. It was a given. How do I accept the fact that it will never happen again? *My spouse died.* That is the first and enormous task of the early weeks.

The second task, which comes just as we are engaging this emotional challenge of our lives, is to have to deal with the countless pragmatic details that come with death. It begins at the funeral home and goes endlessly from there. Each matter must be done properly. Later it will be the legal documents. The will. The estate. Financial matters. Changing names on titles. Changing accounts. Cancelling cards. Notifying companies. And on and on they come.

These two challenges arrive simultaneously in the early weeks. They are the two parallel tracks on which we find ourselves. Emotional and practical. One is of the heart. The other of the head. One emotive, the other cognitive. One is about grief and feelings, the other decisions and actions. Each requires our best. And within each of us there is only so much bandwidth to go around. The ride can be exhausting.

The Night She Died

We knew it was near the end of Karen's life. She was so weak and had not spoken a word that day. Our children came over to see their mother and for all of us to be together. We gathered that evening around Karen's bed, with Patrick and Brooke telling family stories. The three of us would laugh at some funny memory, and Karen, lying there with her eyes closed, could still manage a faint smile. She was aware. She could hear and enjoy those moments.

Eventually, our children and I drifted downstairs so Karen could rest. We were there only a few minutes when, through the monitor, we heard her breathing becoming labored. We rushed back upstairs. I lay down beside her holding her hands. Our children stood at the foot of her bed. She took several loud breaths, with effort. Then four of the softest breaths one could imagine . . . and she was gone.

There are no words. There is no describing those moments, the first moments following such a life-altering event. You know. You remember your loss and the moments that followed. The emptiness. The tears. The emotions swirling. The heart aching. The disorientation as you try to grasp this new reality.

Your world has instantly, radically, permanently changed. You have to put one foot in front of the other in a new world that immediately seems unstable. But you do it. One foot in front of the other. Through the tears. Through the shock. You sit for a moment in your chair and stare at the floor. Looking at nothing but your thoughts and your memories. Feeling a pain you have never known before. A sudden loneliness, like a cold wind sweeping over your soul.

Soon people are talking around you about who needs to be contacted and what needs to be done first. Who will call whom? Who will do what? It's important, of course, but your world as you have known it has just ended. It's over. Your precious partner has died. And your heart is shattered. After all those tears that had come and before all that would follow, you sit there silently without a word. Stunned. Numb. Eyes dry, for the moment. Staring ahead. Silently, slowly trying to take it in. Trying to make sense of what has happened and what it means.

Then someone calls to you. "Dad, what do you think about...?" There is much to do. Slowly you arise out of your chair. One foot in front of the other. There is so much to do. The challenge of the early weeks has begun.

Many Tasks

At just the moment we are so overwhelmed emotionally, there arises this list of tasks demanding our attention. Before us lands an avalanche of all that must be done. The job description of bereaved spouses is mind boggling. Detail after detail, interspersed with much grieving. So much to be accomplished and with only so much capacity. Already fatigued, we begin the climb.

We move ahead. Each duty is important. Each must be successfully engaged. None, no matter how difficult or painful, can be sidestepped, as we are working constantly to survive emotionally. We are drawing on reserves.

Lurking beneath the daunting list of responsibilities is that grief just below the surface. It doesn't take much for it to bubble up. I had to pause in countless conversations to regain my composure. This happened as I was canceling one of Karen's credit cards weeks after she died. "I need to cancel her card because—" and I went silent. "Just a moment, please," my voice cracked as I barely got it out. There was a long pause. And I finally said it. Numerous times some version of this happened. Invariably, the person at the other end of the call was most kind and gracious.

The list of tasks to be done is littered with these emotional landmines. Some errands to run or calls to make touch the open wound of our hearts. We are sent hurtling in tears back to the depth of our grief. Our chest tightens. With effort we take in a deep breath. Our eyes fill. One more time.

One of the early duties was the required trip to Probate Court. The afternoon there was emotionally intense. I was reminded, in the boldest way, that my precious wife had died. As the will was validated, my loss was before me in black and white. Nothing subtle about this. Then I was sworn in as executor, signaling the transition into the rest of my life, without her. That was then, and this is now. The day was powerful.

After that day I was completely spent and, for the first time in many weeks, slept like a rock. That afternoon at court brought a new finality and revision. It was like putting a period at the end of the last sentence of a chapter and then turning the page.

The next morning a weight had fallen off my shoulders. The angst, the turmoil that had churned within me was gone. I remained terribly sad and lonely—which would, of course, be with me for a long time—but I felt a peace. "It is finished," are the words—Jesus's last words spoken from the cross—that came to mind (John 19:30).

That simple act at Court of signing a document and being sworn in as the executor brought to completion in a tangible, real way what my heart had felt and my mind had known. It is finished. I awoke to a new day.

Well, that new day was short-lived. On Sunday I went to the funeral home to pick up copies of Karen's death certificate. Back home, I took it out and actually read it. There it was. Again, in black and white. The tears flowed. The blunt, even brutal, reminder of the reality that I have lost the love of my life.

Such are the days of the early weeks. The emotional swings. The tears and how little it took to trigger them. The grief was that raw.

So many tears—at times it felt like I just couldn't keep up. My grief was producing them faster than I could cry them. Early on, the grief might stay with me through the day, taking its own sweet time. I would be left depleted, exhausted from the sheer effort of it. This is real work. The work of grief.

Different Losses

There are countless losses that go with death. "Ambiguous loss" is the term that points to the more subtle hits we take along the way. Of the major losses in these early weeks of my grief, I found there were three. I would go back and forth, of course, but the sequence tended to be:

Mourning her death—and the sudden emptiness I feel.

Mourning her dying—and the struggle she endured.

Mourning her absence—and the loneliness it brings.

This was how they came over me. I mourned her death, her dying, and then her absence. All of the above. Each of the above. Those were my deepest, earliest wounds.

The Ring

Her death, of course, dominated my focus in the first weeks.
I had just said goodbye to the love of my life. It was always in my
awareness. Usually in the spotlight, but always on the stage of
both my mind and my heart.

For the grieving spouse, so much of what you do in the
first weeks will keep you constantly aware of your fresh wound.
Everything, it seems, is about the death of your life partner—
and often in the most tender ways.

My family and I went for the viewing at the funeral home
the day before Karen's service. The staff handled this time with
respect and dignity. We looked at her body through our tears.
We stood largely in silence, with only an occasional comment.

Then I noticed something very important. Karen's wedding
ring was not on her finger. It turned out simply to have been
an oversight and the man helping us rushed to the back to get
it. With slight embarrassment, he hurriedly returned to the
viewing room to put it back on. As he leaned over the casket,
I said "Wait. Please. I would like to do that myself." So, for the
second time, almost fifty years later, I had the honor of putting
Karen's wedding ring on her finger.

Scattered across the early days are just such reminders of the magnitude of what has happened. Some moments, as this one, will be deeply personal. Others may be more functional. But all will return each of us to the heart of whom we love and all we lost.

Suffering and Relief

Her death dominated my thinking in the early days. Then my focus began gradually to shift from her death to her dying, the final chapter of her life. She had struggled. I began to realize the depth of sadness I had for the ways she suffered. When as positive a person as I have ever known looks up after struggling for weeks and says, "This isn't living," I know that pain has robbed her of life's quality and that the end is now in sight.

I needed to work through the emotional, empathetic ache I felt from the pain she endured.

We both had been so laser-focused medically on getting the job done, there was little time to reflect on what toll this was taking. The awareness of that began to emerge. It also took some time to gain this clarity, because no matter the struggle or pain in her final months, she never lost her smile. Her joy, her positive spirit endured to the end. It was both incredible, and it was deceptive as to just what an ordeal she was engaging. The clarity of my awareness of this began to come into focus. And I mourned. I mourned for her suffering.

Seventeen years before her death, Karen received the diagnosis of breast cancer. Her surgery, radiation, and chemo were successful, and she was cancer-free for the next several years. When it returned, it was now in multiple places. She began treatments and protocols that would continue for the remaining decade of her life. Her medical care was superb, but as time went on her struggle became increasingly difficult.

When I mourn her death, my grief is for me. When I mourn her dying, my grief is for her.

This second phase of my grief helps clarify the first. Yes, I miss her so much and badly want her back. But, no, if she were back, she would still be suffering. I am relieved that struggle is over for her.

Yet, my relief that her suffering has ended in no way cancels out my grief. My grief must be felt and honored and mourned on its own terms. In our temptation to deny the pain of grief, there is always the temptation to sweep it under the rug of relief. I feel relief that her suffering ended *and* mourn the reality that her suffering existed.

Later, three ideas came to me as I was meditating on a Saturday morning. Karen is no longer suffering. She is truly at peace. And I got to spend just over half a century with her. Those are some serious blessings. They take away absolutely none of my grief, but they frame the pain, they give it a context and a broader focus.

I have peace since she has peace.

Seasons of Mourning

"How are you doing?"

"What time is it?"

My emotions could change by the moment. When I was a few weeks out, my mourning came in waves. I got reprieves. Fairly brief ones. A little rest before the next one washed over me. As long as we are still early in our season of mourning, we will continue to feel grief's intensity.

We Heal What We Feel

"I'm doing well." That was my frequent response to friends and acquaintances in public settings who graciously asked in the months following Karen's death. Both they and I knew that it was not a complete sentence. They knew I had stopped because we were in the middle of a social gathering, and this was not a therapy group. "I'm doing well," I said, and I could have added, "under the awful circumstances."

It has been tough. That lady and I were so married. I miss her.

Grief is not something you get over, it's something you live with and work through. I know a bit about working it through, and I'm using what I know. I'm slowly healing. Yes, under the heartbreaking circumstances, I'm doing well.

As we have said, everyone's grief is unique to the relationship, the circumstances, and to their personality. There is no one right way to mourn. There are some unhealthy ways— and denying the pain is the least healthy—but there is not one, correct, prescribed way to do this important work. We must each find our own path, our own way of expressing our grief.

Yet, in spite of this distinctiveness for each of us, there is much we share in common. There are healthy patterns of grief and patterns of mourning that are mutual to us all. In our grief, we share in common the pain of our losses. In our mourning, we share the need to know how to express that pain and why it is important.

Do I enjoy hurting? Of course not. I am hardly masochistic. I do not welcome the emotional ache that is grief. But I do welcome the opportunity to do what I must do in order to feel the joy and fulfillment of being fully alive again. I dislike the simplicity of the phrase "No pain, no gain," but it certainly fits here.

As a pastoral counselor, trained in grief, I know something of the ways to mourn that can bring healing. Knowing how we best grieve is a major plus for all of us as we enter this darkness.

Yet perhaps as important as knowing *how* to engage the grief work is knowing *why* to do the grief work. I am completely confident as I open my heart again and again to the pain of my loss—as I stare into the reality of all that is gone with Karen's death and let my emotions flow—I am confident that what I am doing is healthy and needed and healing. I know as I look at her photo or recall a wonderful memory or visit her grave, though my heart is aching and my tears are streaming, that healing is happening.

I know why to do it—and *that it works*. That is such an advantage. Remember the truth of the adage, "You can't heal what you don't feel." You can't heal what you don't allow yourself to feel and then openly express. I have no control over where my emotions take me, but I do have some say about what I do with

51

those emotions. Feel it and give it a voice. Knowing the wisdom in this, we dare not lack the guts.

To know that, to really understand how healing happens is crucial. If it doesn't facilitate healing, then why on earth would anyone subject themselves to such awful pain? But it does. Mourning brings healing. It's true. So, we muster our courage and open ourselves to another round of heartbreaking grief. This is a valley we can't navigate around or get over—no, we have to take it on directly and go straight through it.

Both Christmas and New Year's Day of that first year were busy with those I love. Though different and often difficult, they went well. When I crashed emotionally were in the days following. I had honored each of these important days enjoyably and often distracted from my grief. When the dust settled and the house was again quiet, her absence came over me like a tidal wave. I cried and could not stop. The pain was raw and unrelenting. She is gone. I will live the rest of my life without her. I had known that, but now I *feel* it.

Taking a Break

Grief is exhausting.

Let's pause for a moment here. In fact, for me pausing for a moment every so often is essential to have the strength for the task of mourning. I believe it's true for us all.

We need rest. We need a break. We need moments to renew and restore.

Every so often, when I want to give more direct guidance to a counseling client, I will playfully ask, "May I run your life for just a moment?" We will laugh, and I then offer my input. So, may I run your life for just a moment? Thanks.

This is what I encourage you to do:

Choose the activities and relationships that will give you the life and energy you will need for the job at hand. Be purposeful in those choices. Then linger there. Enjoy them. Take your time.

This is not denial. It is a moment of deliberate distraction to take good care of youself and to give youself the energy for the work that is ahead. Allow yourself to be restored.

Remember the basics of healthful self-care during stressful times:

Keep a normal routine.
Get rest. Exercise. Eat healthfully.

Stay engaged with those who are especially good for you.

Develop your community.

Express your emotions in ways that work for you.

Do those activities that enrich you and give you energy.

Keep your spiritual life—meditation, prayer, reading—a priority.

Do something meaningful each day.

Read a book you enjoy. Listen to the music you love.

Go for walks.

And be true to who you are.

Bring your best to this challenging season. The journey all but requires it.

Mourning Her Absence

Absence is another loss. Paradoxically, it is the palpable *presence of her absence*. I so badly wanted her here. She should be here. Her absence was not just a void but a presence of its own. I know how crazy that must sound to those who have never felt it—and how much sense it makes to those who have.

Karen's death and her ongoing absence in my life are two different losses. I have long known, from those who research grief, that it often takes spouses years to mourn their partners' deaths. Why so long? Because it's the "loss that keeps on losing." They may have died at an earlier point in time, but their absence continues.

As I heal my grief from her death bit by bit, I am still left with the day-by-day awareness of her not being with me. Every day I have to live with her absence anew. I came across this journal entry from the spring following Karen's death: "This morning I saw the most magnificent cherry blossoms in my neighbor's yard just as the sun was rising—and felt such a sadness. I cannot describe how beautiful they are, and how much joy Karen would have had in seeing the landscape covered in pink. I can just hear her. Only I can't."

The emotion is loneliness. Often, it's not the grief of her death that is front and center in my heart, it's her being gone. It is her absence that creates the unsettling quiet in my home and the void in my heart. It's the loneliness.

A terrible storm came through in the early morning hours knocking out power to the house a couple of months after Karen's passing. It was the longest, quietest, emptiest day. Barely a sound the whole day. The silence and stillness brought home for me just how alone I felt. It brought back the awareness of the quiet. The house becoming absolutely silent. From sheer loneliness, I cried as hard that day as I had cried since she died.

Karen died during the pre-vaccine period of the COVID-19 pandemic, so there was little socializing after her death. The loneliness I felt was both for her and for my friends. The distinction between the two was pretty clear. The sharp pain of loneliness was for her. The dull ache was for my community. It was clear which dominated my emotional landscape. The haunting quiet of the house kept reminding me.

Yet, I am beginning to carve out my new life—playing the hand I'm dealt. I don't like it one bit. It's lonely. It's empty. Yes, I have a good life, but I have no Karen to see and with whom I can talk and enjoy.

Balance. It feels like I'm off balance emotionally. I realize how intertwined our lives had become. I naturally, intuitively turn to her countless times over these weeks in ways she had always been lovingly there for me—to ask her or tell her something—and no Karen. There is something unnatural about what had become second nature no longer being true. So empty. So lonely.

There is so much meaning missing from doing life together. Karen is not here to share it. It was such a joy to live life together.

Joyful Spirit

Many years ago, our family of four was at our local yogurt shop, each enjoying a cup with our favorite flavors as we sat at our table. Next door was a fitness center, and frequently those in gym clothes would come in after their workouts.

After a few minutes of enjoying our yogurt, a huge man came in and walked past our table. I had never seen someone so big or muscles so ripped. Playfully and sarcastically, I turned to my teenage son sitting next to me and said, "Hey, Patrick, go tell that punk that I could clean his plow."

Without missing a beat, Karen added, "Yes, Patrick, and then see if he has any other farm implements your daddy could work on."

Karen and I laughed so hard that the children, thoroughly embarrassed, went outside the shop to finish their yogurt.

She was delightful. And that kind of joyful spirit is one of many reasons the loss is so deep.

We are each keenly aware of the connection between the depth of our love and the intensity of our grief. The more we loved, the more we lost.

The Way Forward

As the weeks continued on this journey, the pain was no longer as *acute* or as *constant*. It became *deep* and *consistent*.

There are days when something may remind me of Karen and tears fill my eyes. Early after her death it happened constantly. Whether prompted by a specific trigger or not, the tears were always there. Now, months after her death, I know I can go there and have the cry that's coming, or not.

As the months and years go by, it is often a choice. And almost always I choose to go. I always remain open for engaging my still-healing broken heart. I know the value of the journey through that valley. I know the healing that comes.

I take a deep breath and let the feelings flow.

I know there is a way forward. At several months out, I just can't see it yet. My vision is limited to only the few steps ahead. I can feel it. I know if I continue down this dark, painful path it will be there. One day.

There is not yet a light at the end of this tunnel. I am not drawn forward because I see it. I am drawn forward because I believe it is there. I move ahead because, in spite of the present darkness, in spite of my wandering through this wilderness of my grief, I believe that one day it will be a new day. I believe that healing will come. I believe that's called faith. The conviction that there is a resurrection beyond struggle, heartache, and death.

Listening to Anger

An emotion often privately felt with grief is anger. It may be aimed in any number of directions—at God for letting this happen, at our loved one for dying, at ourselves or the medical staff for not having done more. The anger is often irrational in its focus, but there is a rationale behind it.

You see, anger is a meta-emotion, which means an emotion in response to other emotions. No matter how deeply we feel it, anger is not a primary emotion. Think of the primary colors. Blue + yellow = green. Similarly, hurt + fear = anger. Hurt from the past plus fear of the future creates anger in the present.

Listen to your anger, should you feel it. Use it for clarity and insight. Listen for what it is saying, look to what is beneath it. Look for the hurt, which is likely rather apparent. The pain for most of us is the ache of the death itself. But then there are the many other dimensions of loss that accompany our loved one's passing—the dreams never to be realized, the moments never to be shared.

Which then takes us to our fears, the other half of the anger formula. Of what are we afraid now that we are alone?

By what challenges do we feel intimidated? What anxieties lurk beneath the passion of our anger? Take the time and the effort to identify them. Only then can we most successfully address them. Use the anger as a call to meet these needs, to heal the hurts, and attend to the fears.

Forgive Yourself

Regret is yet another emotion of the bereaved. Things said or left unsaid. Things done or left undone. Those memories sting since there is nothing we now can do about them. We can no longer apologize or talk through the unfortunate words spoken. The day is passed that we can express the words of love or appreciation that may have been overlooked and left unsaid. They were our spouses, our life partners. We adored them. And on occasions, we can recall with painful clarity when we let them down.

Karen was diagnosed with cancer many years before her death. Earlier, we knew it was possible cancer could take her life, and later that it was probable. We used the advance notice to our advantage. We were intentional about doing the things we wanted to do and seeing many of the places we wanted to experience. There was little we wanted to express to each other that was unspoken. We were fortunate in that this left us with few regrets of things unspoken or left undone.

But every now and then a reminder comes along of something overlooked, something forgotten. And now it's too late. There was a precious poem to which Karen introduced me from her childhood. I loved it, and I loved the playful, childlike way Karen recited it. You couldn't help but laugh out loud at the sheer joy of her inflection.

A handful of years ago I told her that we must record her saying it, so our grandchildren would always have this poem in their grandmother's voice to hear and to play for their children. They would love to have it. I reflected on this in my journal entry almost two months after her death with these words, "The years passed. Today, for the first time since then, I thought of Karen's poem. Time had moved on. We got busy with life, and we forgot. It completely slipped my mind. Until today."

Regrets. Some big. Some small, but big enough to sting. Possibilities for joy, expressions of love we left on the table. Several weeks after she died, I was going through some files and found a card I bought for her, perhaps two or three years before. It was a beautiful card expressing how much she meant to me. I had tucked it away to give to her. I then completely forgot about it. The discovery of it hurt my heart. I thought it. I bought it. But I never gave it to her. She never knew the joy of receiving it.

Please don't ignore your memories, those times of regret. Intentional forgiveness will likely be in order. You and I are fallible human beings. We make mistakes. I would encourage us all to do two things with those regrets—whether they are those said or unsaid, done or left undone. First, consciously forgive yourself. Say it out loud, if you like, but be sure to mean it. You are human, and you messed up. You dropped the ball. Forgive yourself.

Then, decide—whatever the misstep—that you will forever use it as a life lesson. You may make other mistakes, but you will be deliberate about trying never to make that one again. To those who matter to you, say what you want to say to them, and do what you want to do for them. Let there be as few regrets as possible. Let the lesson learned be the new frame in which you put that memory. Use it, as you grow wiser and evermore considerate.

Yearning

Two months after Karen died a friend told me of being at an elegant resort, having drinks at the end of the day. At six o'clock a bagpiper stepped onto the veranda and began to play beautiful Scottish music. Immediately I thought, "I have to take Karen there." Two months. Yes, two months after her death that whole thought, about taking her to this resort, crossed my mind before the obvious hit me.

I know a part of this is simply habit. Five decades together will create one. Neurologists refer to the preference the brain has to habits, to previous life experience over new information. This implicit knowledge of the relationship and presence of those we dearly love is deeply encoded at the subconscious level in our minds. Though our conscious minds are keenly aware that our spouses have died, the years of encoding are too strong to readily change.

What is true of the brain is also true of the heart. When it comes to any reality we profoundly do not want, complete acceptance is a process. We resist it. It is one thing to *know it* and another *fully to accept it*. This is not denial as much as it is resistance—not wanting it to be true.

You may well experience the same thing with your loss. We push against what we know is true—both because of our cognitive wiring and because we so badly don't want it to be so. Thus, the process of mourning our loss often takes a long, long time. For the mourner, this can be brutal—but vitally important. Begin to accept the reality.

I thought I had. But, again, complete acceptance is a process. About nine months after her death, I had two dreams which clearly spoke to this. I have always thought of dreams as coming from the subconscious, from the deepest places within our hearts and souls. The dream itself is a drama acted out to convey a message from that depth to our conscious minds. It is a reality of which our souls want us to be aware.

In the first dream I was following Karen through a maze with twists and turns. Then the hallway came to an end with a hole cut into the wall. It was just large enough for Karen to squeeze through, which she did. As I approached it, the opening had become even smaller. I told her there was no way I could get through it. "If I try, I'll get stuck," I called out to her. As I said this, I had the sense she was still moving ahead. Desperately I called to her, pleading, "Please, please come back!!" At that moment I was jolted awake, panicked.

What feels like part two of the same dream came about a month later. Clearly there was a powerful message being conveyed. The message was relentless, not giving up until I got it. It shows how deeply I was resisting giving her up. Early on that morning a month later I awoke from a dream in which I was imploring her to come back. "I want you back so badly," I said to her. "I will do whatever you need from me. I'll do anything I can if you will please come back."

There was a moment of quiet, and then in the dream Karen said simply, "Ron, I didn't leave you. I died."

I would say that is pretty clear. The yearning for her within my heart had not truly accepted the painful reality or my dream life would not have wasted my time at rest with the consistent, burning message that she is gone. Beyond my reach.

I knew it was true. No, really, I did. I just didn't want it to be true. So badly I didn't want it to be true.

"I died," she said. Yes, I understand. Finally. So, these dreams ended.

A footnote to the dreams: The comment I made in the first dream about not trying to follow her through the hole in the wall, "If I try, I'll get stuck," may be important. I wonder if the message was: if I don't let go of Karen, accept her death, mourn the loss, then I will be *stuck in my grief* and never fully heal or move on with my life. I wonder. Because it's true.

Goodness

Expect to feel guilty.

It may be when you laugh out loud. Or realize what a fun evening you spent with friends. Or that you really felt good that day.

You may feel guilty, because, well, how dare you! Your precious spouse has died and you are enjoying your life. Don't be surprised.

Expect to feel it. The guilt. The awkwardness. The contradiction of feeling anything like joy at a time of heartache.

I remember the first time I laughed after Karen died. I have dear friends. Some are hilarious. In their company, at times, I am simply the audience, and a most entertained audience. I was that night. I laughed as we carried on with our foolishness. My goodness, how I needed that! And, my goodness, how strange it felt on reflection as I drove home.

Or someone may casually ask how I'm doing. I respond with, "I'm doing really well. Thank you," and realize the new and distinctive lilt in my voice.

Understand that you will feel good again, and you may flinch instinctively the first times you do.

Both Worlds

The pendulum keeps swinging. From the ache to the relief. From the past to the present. From the pain to the hope. From what was to what is—and even to what may be. The pendulum swings between these parallel lives we lead.

Mourning brings healing. As always, the healing is slow. It is a slow and unsteady process. It is a bumpy road. Healing involves the mending of the wound. Healing increasingly opens the door to the possibility of a new life.

I think of the image of the scales of justice as a metaphor. On one side is the grief of my loss. On the other is my new life. I begin the journey with the scales decidedly weighed on the side of my grief. Slowly. Ever so slowly the scales begin shifting. My focus had been strongly weighed to the past. Now it is beginning to balance to the present, to my life now. There is some resistance, for it requires "leaving" my wife. Her spirit goes with me, but she does not.

It occurred to me later that when Karen said in different contexts in the last year or so of her life "don't look back" she likely was guiding me—knowing that I would be here, without her. Steering me to live in the present. Then to look ahead, to carve out a meaningful life, and move into it. Do all the work. Grieve my heart out—begin to heal—then move forward, not back. It is a process. And it takes its sweet time.

This is a time of the ebb and flow. I was embarking on my new life and walked in a local store to buy a new frying pan. Yes, a frying pan. How emotionally neutral is that? It's not. There I stand in the kitchen section of the store. Hardly my home turf. All I can think of is Karen and how she should be there with me. A kind salesperson comes up to me and asks if she can help. I begin to speak, and tears fill my eyes. I can't stop them. Somehow, I struggled out the words, "My wife died." She gently said, "I'll give you a moment," and stepped away.

This whole movement forward happens in fits and starts. One moment I'm enthusiastic about a project in this new phase of my life and the next I'm in tears looking at frying pans. Such is life in the season of healing. Ebbs and flows. This is what healing is like. As the pendulum swings, make sure your seat belt is securely fastened.

On rereading my journal entries, I found an interesting pattern. Once enough time had passed, I would describe a good day in which the words "enjoyed" or "meaningful" or even "peaceful" might be used. Then, consistently, the following paragraph would begin with decidedly transitional phrases like "And then," or "Then *boom*," as some trigger would happen sending me over the emotional cliff. The descent into mourning can be severe and rapid. One moment I may be feeling pretty good, and the trigger, whatever it is, sends me back into my grief.

Expect the pendulum to swing. Remember, it's healthy. It's healing. It's inevitable. We are always tempted to equate what is painful with what is bad. This is a good hurt. It allows me to do more of the work I must do if I am to heal. With the awareness that this healing takes a long time, please keep the balance in focus—between continuing to mourn and carving out your new life.

For many, as soon as they feel some relief from the intensity of their grief, they try to put their pain aside and hope never to feel it again. They often call it *closure*, and there is no such thing as final closure. It's not closure. It's repression, and it isn't healthy.

Earlier the grief was so intense they had no choice. When you get to the time when you do have a choice, I encourage you to always choose to let the pendulum swing. Engage your on-going grief. Then develop your new life with its emerging possibilities. When that pendulum has swung from your grief to your current life, do not be shy about enjoying it for all its worth. Savor the moments. Savor each relationship. Savor every positive experience.

Just as we know our mourning is healthy, please know that relishing the present—and the blessings that remain—is equally healthy. And it is even necessary for our healing to go well. We need a break from the pain, from the exhausting task of grief.

We need to have some energy coming *in* for a change, with so much going out. This is not denial; it's wholesome distraction. Taking a break. Renewing. Please consciously, intentionally, enjoy the life that is before you and the relationships that are there for you.

Stay in contact with both worlds.

A Good Life
with Lots of Tears

Months following my wife's death, I found that my grief was consistently present. It was not always center stage, in the spotlight, but it was at least in the background. Even as the pendulum swings to the other side, it remains in my awareness. That may be true for you as well. It doesn't mean you are not healing. It means healing takes a long time. I found where I had written in my journal, almost a year later, the words, "Perhaps tomorrow I will again make headway in organizing and planning my new life. But today I will mourn that my former life couldn't continue just a little longer."

As we honor our grief and keep it current, we will notice changes. Think of our mourning as ocean waves coming in and washing over us. If we will acknowledge each painful wave and give that feeling expression, we will begin to notice a pattern of change in three different ways. The waves of grief will come in less frequently, will hit less powerfully, and will recede more readily.

I leaned into my pain. I mourned my grief. I am healing. I am moving forward. I remember a painful recollection I had had many months into this journey, and I ached from the memory. I ached. I *only* ached. It wasn't a piercing into my heart. It hurt, but it hurt less severely. I am healing, slowly healing.

I shall always remember Karen's birthday, the first without her, several months after her death. The tears flowed readily down my cheeks. Yet they came, not from a place of raw grief, but from a place in my heart of deep tenderness and loss. It was a most tender day with plenty of tears. But it was one in which I was aware that I was healing. My mourning remained current. It was a regular part of my life, but my life was not dominated by it. I continued to build my new life as one who was mourning his loss but was not defined by it. It may sound like a kind of oxymoron, but I experienced it as *a good life with lots of tears*.

In countless ways, the days were good days. I felt connected with her spirit of joy and knew she would want me to. There were many good moments—not great moments, as they were when she was here, but good. Really good. I reset the bar, for now, on what I can expect of the quality of my life. Good is good. I dared not expect more any time soon. Good is good.

The World That Is

The timing on everything in this process varies from one person to another. But each grieving spouse will remember when they began carving out their new life. We develop schedules and routines that work for us. We rearrange things in our homes. We slowly adjust to being alone. We are a family of one in a house that now may feel too big for only one.

There were times when I began enjoying more and more of my life, the new patterns of the day, the minor accomplishments of doing for myself what Karen had always done for us. There was a subtle moment that stood out to me. I realized I wanted to start writing again. Aside from my counseling, what had given me purpose in life before Karen died was my writing. I wanted to start again. For the previous months, what had been my life was caring for her and then mourning her death. Months later, I came to a new place, having worked through so much. I was ready to write. Some of the fog had lifted, and I could again see beyond my next three steps.

As I worked, I felt true happiness for many days in a row. Make no mistake, the loneliness was still there. I missed Karen deeply—the companionship, the connection, the conversation, the laughter. I missed it all. But I had times of real happiness.

My life had meaning. This fulfilled life sits beside—not in contradiction with—my loneliness. They are partners as I move forward. I develop my new patterns and interests while I continue to mourn the loss. As I sit here reflecting on it, it amazes (and pleases) me that they are not in contradiction to each other. They are simply different parts of my whole life. I can have a great time with friends, and then I can break down in tears. Both are genuine. Both are me.

Earlier, this was not true. My grief dominated the entire landscape of life and of my days. Where I am now shows I am healing. I have moved from acute grief to sorrow. The sorrow is a sadness that will be with me for a long time. It is a response to her absence, to all the moments of warmth and joy we can no longer share. But grief had dominated. Sorrow has its painful place in my heart but allows me to move forward with renewed purpose.

As I will often repeat, the process of healing takes its time. We inch along. But we are getting traction. As we engage the grief, we move forward. More and more days will be "good days." Brighter. Lighter. We will increasingly be more in charge of the quality of these days. We will continue to refine our new routines, adding activities we enjoy and find fulfilling.

As we move forward, we will intuitively continue nesting in our homes and in our new lives. Though a part of me early on felt like I was dishonoring Karen—or at least her memory—this is becoming *my* new life in *my* house, as I move ahead. One day I was talking with my daughter and her son William. I was wondering what to do with some household belongings, and my seven-year-old grandson spoke up, "It's your stuff. Do what you want to with it." It's my life. I am beginning to do what I want to with it. The freedom to do so—not the circumstances that got me here—feels solid.

During the early months of my grief, I found myself, on occasion, compulsively getting things done. Straightening up a room. Organizing my desk. Ordering my schedule for the day. Now understand, this is not a contradiction to my personality, but these times it seemed excessive. Then it dawned on me. As I am mourning, I am looking directly into the loss, the upheaval, the emotional disorder of my life. I couldn't stand chaos in both of my worlds—internally and externally. I had to create order in the only place in my life I could.

Another facet of this transition is in the evolving focus of our losses. The death of our spouses will go from being a cloud that casts its shadow of grief over every area of our lives, to being now reduced to its own area. Though it is still real grief and pain, it is now one part of a much larger life.

Earlier, everything was seen through the lens of her death and her absence. Each experience of my days was lived under the darkness of that shadow. But then slowly life became lighter. We value our friendships, our homes, brisk walks, our new lives without that cloud hovering over every moment of it. If ever you feel guilty about this, and you well may, remember that you are guilty of nothing. You are living the new life you have been given, not the one of your choosing, the best you can.

Slowly the world that was is being replaced by the world that is. My new world by myself and without Karen became ingrained into my intuitive awareness. I had such mixed feelings about this, but I no longer expect her to be there. Increasingly I don't have to remind myself that Karen won't be walking to the doorway to tell or ask me something. Slowly, with pain and deep regret, no longer do I anticipate her to appear with that beautiful smile. When I was continuing to live intuitively in the former world, I was consistently jolted back into the awareness of my new reality—she is not here and she won't be. I am no longer jolted, at least in that way. I now live here. Without her.

I have leaned into my pain. I have mourned my grief. I am moving forward. Healing happens. Not quickly. Not painlessly. But it is happening.

He Read the Book

Karen and I lost our two-year-old son Eric in an automobile accident many years ago. Eric had left some toys—including his precious Snoopy—at his grandparents' house on his last visit. Before they saw him again Eric died. What should she do with his toys, his grandmother wondered. She couldn't give them back to grieving parents. That would seem cruel. She wouldn't think of throwing them away.

So, she took his toys, placed them in a cabinet, and locked it shut. It was all too fresh—she would decide later what to do with them. Years would go by—twenty-three, in fact. During this time Grandma died.

I had written a book on grief based on our experience following Eric's death. It had just been published as we went to visit Grandpa. Copies of the book were given to each in the family. It was a warm, tender moment together as we each remembered quietly the ordeal we had engaged as a family.

One of Eric's uncles took his book home and read all of it the evening he got it. As a man who acknowledges he rarely reads or cries, he did both that Saturday evening.

My wife Karen and I saw him again Sunday morning before we left to drive home. We stood in the kitchen together, and he did a very personal and courageous thing. He gently spoke of not knowing what we had needed following the death of our son. "We didn't know what to do. We didn't know whether to talk with you about Eric or not? So, we decided it would be best not to."

He had read my book carefully and thoughtfully. With a look of pure relief on his face, he continued, "Now I see we are *supposed* to talk about him."

He then talked of Eric. He remembered playing with him on the floor, having him climb up his legs, and the memories from all of us went on and on. It was a rich, wonderful time as we remembered—aloud—together.

Later Eric's uncle asked me to come with him out to Grandpa's office. From the desk he took a key and opened a cabinet I had never noticed. He reached in and—to my amazement—pulled out some of our son's most precious belongings. Karen and I had no idea what had happened to Eric's Snoopy. It simply had been one of our many losses.

"Mama didn't know what to do with these," he said. "She wanted them to be kept safe. So, she locked them away. Eric left them on his last visit."

I was overwhelmed. I hope I made some sense in how I responded. We had given up seeing anything else of Eric's two decades ago. And now, here was his Snoopy and his well-worn puppet.

That morning had been such a tender and beautiful moment.

A part of Eric's memory had been tenderly locked away for years both in a pine cabinet and in our hearts. "We didn't know what to do," his uncle said—and as soon as he did know, so much was unlocked. The memories and the stories and the love flowed.

"We didn't know what to do," he said.

I encourage all who are reading this book to talk with those around them. To those who mean the most to you. Tell them what you need. Tell them how they can best love you. Tell them how and when you need for them to be with you.

Then the memories and the stories and the love can flow.

Life in the Singular

I remember when I first saw it in writing. I received a document from my auto insurance company. Beside my name it read, "Marital Status: Widowed." I knew well that my wife had died, but I had not yet thought of the word "widowed." My identity was changing.

We shared a life together. The two of us. We were a team. Now I run onto the playing field each day as the whole team. It feels strange. Awkward. Off-balance. Lonely. Something fundamental to my life was missing. Somehow, I had to get into a new balance. I had to learn how to be me without we.

Over time, I began to feel like I really did live by myself. I was no longer half of a couple. My identity was shifting to my new reality. I was no longer the person I had been. I lost my wife, our lives together, and something of who I had been—as I move from who I was to who I am becoming. Without the influence of her company and the presence of her companionship, I well may develop new interests and explore new paths in this uncharted world of mine. I will be looking for what brings purpose and meaning and fulfillment to me *now*.

The other half of *we* is gone. I am having to figure out how I am going to be whole again. A part of that is learning how to buy towels and cook and wash clothes on the delicate cycle, but most of it is about identity. I am learning to think of myself as the new person I am now. The two became one. Now one has to become one. That is a whole new identity.

This issue comes into sharp focus with the awkwardness of using either the singular or plural. It has always been *our* home. Now it is mine alone. *My* home. The singular was slow in coming. Something about it didn't feel right. Habit, as always, was a factor in making a change. But it also felt somehow like a betrayal—of Karen's rightful place and of the place I wanted her to be. Like leaving her out of where she belonged. Saying *my* home felt like speaking a truth I didn't want to be true. But it is now *mine* no matter how much I want it to be *ours*.

This journey is about healing from the wound of the loss— but it is, as well, about beginning to make the most of our new world. If we often feel fatigued, we should. As we mourn, we also are engaging the transformation of our lives.

My identity began changing. I was easing forward, sometimes at the pace of a crawl, reclaiming myself as a whole on my own. For each of us who mourn, our identity has been, in part, that of a spouse. But there is more to who we are. It's time to expand the rest of us.

Towels

One afternoon, I was at a home goods store. I needed new towels. What a joke. My presence there defined the phrase being *out of one's element*. What size? What color? What design? What maker? What was I doing there?

I walked over to the towel section. It felt like a canyon. Towels were stacked up on every wall to almost twice my height. The solids were in every color. The patterns had every design. There was no shortage of options. But there was a shortage of expertise.

I left. I will return soon with a coach.

The other half of *we* is gone. I am having to figure out how I am going to be whole again. A part of that is learning how to buy towels and cook and wash and shop, but most of it is about self-identity. I am learning to think of myself as the new person I am now.

We each had our specialties that came with our informal job descriptions. Now I specialize in everything. I am not whining, merely acknowledging that this is different, and there will be a learning curve. A learning curve with my new job description and with my new marital status. With what I do and with who I am. I'm having to get up to speed. And I am getting up to speed, with the support in countless ways of those who mean the world to me.

So much changes with the loss of a spouse. But, then, you knew that. It's a part of that far-reaching transition to which I keep referring. So many, many changes. In what we do and who we are.

Oh, and they are navy blue. The new towels. A beautiful navy blue, extra-large. A little coaching from good friends means a lot.

Side by Side

The window in my study looks down the hill to the street below and then up toward a beautiful grove of pines and oaks beyond. When I pause in my reading or writing, I instinctively look up to enjoy the view. Regularly, I will see someone walking past. Our neighborhood is self-contained, with little traffic, so it is a natural place for walkers from surrounding neighborhoods to venture over and get their healthful miles in.

I looked up today and saw an older man, whom I have seen many times, walking by. He always wears the same stylish hat to block the sun's rays. I don't know who he is, but I know what to expect next. And so, I continued to look. A few seconds later his wife came into view. I have seen them countless times, and she is always walking several steps behind her husband in their nearly identical hats. They are consistently the same distance apart. Never walking together, always a few yards apart.

You know how little things in life can capture your attention? This couple did, for a special reason. I began seeing them some time ago. It was about the time Karen could no longer walk with me. The cancer and its treatments had compromised her strength and stamina.

You know the question I always wonder when I see them. Why are they not walking together? Side by side. Sharing the moments. Even holding hands. Make no mistake, there is likely an excellent reason they walk apart, and it must work well for them. I trust it does. I am not being judgmental toward them. I'm just feeling lonely for me. They are simply a reminder of what can no longer be in my life.

I would love to be able to put on my walking shoes, as Karen puts on hers, and take her hand and walk our paths together. Side by side. Talking, laughing. Sharing the day and the beauty of God's world.

These little things we see remind us of the big ones we feel. Of what we can no longer do. Of those with whom we can no longer do them. They remind us of all that we had and all that we lost.

Mourning is tough. And the reminders are all around.

My First Trip

Two years after Karen died, I traveled for the first time. COVID-19, of course, had restrained all of us, but there had been no eagerness in me for traveling alone. I had accepted a speaking engagement at Hilton Head Island and decided to take the following week off and stay on the Atlantic coast. I would visit with friends who had moved to various places on the coastline of South Carolina and Georgia. It could be a good, relaxing time.

I had no way of knowing how present Karen would be in my awareness. In the hours on the road with little distraction and only music in the background, I realized how vivid the memories of her were with me. Rarely had I traveled without her. There were two times on this trip I especially missed her. When I saw something familiar. And when I saw something new. Yes, I missed her all the time.

The new experiences were expected. These are the countless times we all turn to our partner and say, "Oh, look at that . . . " I would still feel the impulse, lo these many, many months later, to want to show it to Karen. There was no surprise there. I have long read of how those deeply encoded neural connections in our brain are slow to update.

The Quiet House

What caught me by surprise were not the new experiences, but the impact of seeing the familiar. Before me were the sights and the places to which we had been countless times over the years. But this was the first time without her. This was the first time I had ridden through the countryside of South Georgia or walked the majestic streets of Savannah or strolled down the pier at Saint Simons Island…alone. I went past Sea Island where we spent our honeymoon. I stayed at the hotel on Saint Simons where we often vacationed and stepped onto the beach where we walked countless times. Other than the delightful breaks catching up with dear friends over dinners along the coast, I was feeling as alone as I had ever felt.

The aloneness was familiar, however. It took me back to that first Thanksgiving without Karen, when the house was so quiet. Each experience on this week-long journey was a "first," just as that was my first holiday without her. Each was my first time at a familiar site without her there. This entire coastal trip itself was setting after setting of visiting places we had always known together. It felt empty. Lonely. My heart and my mind still associate those places with our being together.

What I came to realize was how important having these *first experiences* was to healing. It brought a reframe to any place or setting we had always known together. Having done it once. Then twice. Then…over time, it ever-so-gradually became a part of my new life. With profound regret, my new life without her.

90

Do I miss her in those settings? Of course. Is it lonely without her? Of course, it is. Does it still sting walking into those familiar places? Not as much. Not quite as much. Not after the ache of the first few times. Whatever the site or the experience, it is now placed in the broader setting of my new life in my new world.

Languishing

I have a feeling every so often. As I write this, I am now many months on this path. Significant healing has happened. The constant intensity of my grief has subsided. I am involved in my life, in activities and relationships. I am busy.

Then I slowly begin to feel something. No, that's not quite right. I slowly begin *not to feel* much of anything. My senses are flat. Feeling very little. I may go through the day simply going through the motions. It's not depression. I feel nothing. And it doesn't feel good. It's called *languishing*.

Languishing is a sense of emptiness, of stagnation. It's to feel nothing, nothing of the richness of life, the joy, the meaning. Nor is it to feel sadness or grief. Languishing can come from different origins, out of different contexts. But for me, in the context of my grief journey, it comes from having gotten distracted, from having lost touch with my heart. I had gotten too busy and subconsciously capped off the pain of my loss that was begging to be expressed. My grief was backing up and needing to be released.

I was first aware of it decades ago following the death of our son. Months afterward, I felt this emptiness. Not grief. Not sadness. Feeling nothing. Then it dawned on me. I had not actively mourned in some time. With no conscious awareness, I had distanced myself from my emotions.

One evening, I was driving home about dusk as I approached Eric's cemetery, which I passed each day. I pulled in, walked to his grave, and the tears flowed that were begging to come out. It was one of those transforming moments reconnecting me with my love for my son and with my deepest, truest self. I finished my trip home exhausted and relieved. The emptiness was gone. I was in touch with me again. I had given a voice to the grief that needed to be expressed.

Languishing. The feeling that comes when we don't allow ourselves to feel all that we feel. We're not intentionally repressing emotions—we're getting distracted and not intentionally expressing them. To each of us who did not grow up in touch with our emotions, be aware. Be intentionally aware. When you feel the emptiness, when you are feeling nothing, when you are languishing, be aware. Open your heart and let your healing grief emerge.

The First Anniversary

All of the firsts are emotionally tough, but the first anniversary of Karen's death was awful. It began with tears. There were tears throughout the day. It was awful. But something happened that day. Maybe even a transformation. I think so. I came out at a different place.

The most poignant moment came at the very end of the day. Karen died just after 9:30 in the evening. On the anniversary of that evening, I went to the bedroom in which she had been sleeping to have a seat and ride it out. I remembered the events of the year before.

I relived it all as I sat there on that first anniversary—on the evening and at the very moment of that evening that she took those final breaths. Nothing could hurt more than the night it happened. But, in a different way, this came close. The tears flowed.

The moment of her death arrived. The moment passed. And it was over. My tears slowly subsided. I sat there in that quiet, dark room lighted only from the light in the hallway. It was then that something happened changing the course of this journey. In the quiet of those few moments, I realized how I now felt. I said it out loud, "I am alone."

In the entire year since her passing I had never felt quite that way, quite that alone. It was an awareness that simply and suddenly came over me. Now, I had not been delusional for those twelve months—I knew she was not here. But not in this way. This was different. "I am completely alone." Around me all I sensed was stillness. It was not frightening. Not at all. There was nothing there of which to be afraid. I was completely alone.

I struggle to express this adequately. Her dying, her suffering had permeated our home and my heart for the past year. I would see her in my memory and feel her struggling as the cancer raged. The pain. The ordeal. "This isn't living," she had said in her final days. My heart ached for her as she lived it and the anguish continued during those months following her death, as I remembered over and over. And now, shortly before ten o'clock on the first anniversary of her death it was over. Somehow, I let it go. I let her go. For I was alone, unlike any time before. It was not by choice. It simply came into my awareness. Perhaps my contribution was having paved the way by mourning as completely and fully as I knew how for the past year. I sat in the dark and said, "I am alone."

I will continue to mourn, to be sure. I have still lost Karen, and my heart will ache as I miss her. I will continue to mourn, but my focus is now on her life more that her death. I have let her go.

I looked at that gorgeous picture of her as I was about to leave my office the afternoon following this first anniversary. I picked it up to see her closely. "I got to be with her," were the words I instinctively whispered, feeling so blessed. Up to this day, I know I would have said, because I often had, "I lost her. Just look at all I've lost." Not this time. "I got to be with her," were my words.

I am letting her suffering go, for she is at peace. I am letting my longing go, for she is at rest.

My focus is less on Karen's death than on her life. Less on what I have lost than what I have lived.

Less on how she *was* with me and more on how her spirit *goes* with me. Less on my past and more on being present. Less on where I've been than where I'm going.

Now I am living more in the present, looking to the future, and thankful for the past.

Scattered Showers

In the early months, the pain was *acute* and *constant*. Then it became *deep* and *consistent*. And now, with more healing, it has become *tender* and *periodic*.

The tenderness we feel in response to our loss will always be with us. Each of us was that much in love. The wound will become a scar, but that place, that loss in our hearts will always be tender to the touch. We will feel it with any number of reminders that trigger that sensitive place. Moments of sadness will be with us forever. We will continue to open our hearts and shed our tears.

I have often referred to my tearful moments as my scattered showers. I may have been having a good time, and something triggered my sadness. I have my moment, my shower, and then I go back to enjoying my life again.

This tenderness does not inhibit us from moving forward. There is a life ahead, one that our spouses, who could not continue this journey with us, would want us to live fully and abundantly. We press on. We take out our pens, turn the page, and begin to write the next chapter of our lives.

This is resiliency. We get up and with a newfound strength move ahead seeking a life with purpose, meaning and times of joy. You and I have been out of control of so much that matters, it may feel that we have precious little control over anything. We had no say in our losses, but we have ultimate say over how we respond to it.

We can make healthful choices.

A life of fulfillment following a profound loss is virtually always found in those who are clear they retain a measure of power in how they respond to those events. We cannot control the wind and the sea, but we do have sails and rudders that make us the captains of much of our fate.

This reframe takes with deep seriousness the magnitude of the loss. It acknowledges the power of, first, engaging the grief, and then assuming control of the parts of our lives over which we retain authority. We may not have power over everything, but we are not going to give away the power over the life we do have.

Making the Best
of This Day

I remember the transition. Gradually, my focus shifted. Increasingly, it was on how I would make the best of each day. The change was not a decision I made; it was a discovery I realized. I was getting more accustomed to my new life.

I was at a new place in my grief. It was still alive and needing to be tended. But when I felt the pain and sensed the tears I was saddened, though no longer overwhelmed. I wept but was not consumed. It was no longer a tidal wave. I feel it. I honor it. I give voice to it. I express it. I work through it. As difficult as it is, I am then ready to reengage my day.

I began to awaken in the morning, not with the thought I had been cheated out of another day with Karen, but with the intent to make the best of the day I had been given. It was what it was—a day of blessings and losses, and I would make it the most meaningful and fulfilling day I could.

The days felt lighter. Some of the burden lifted.

This is my new world. I have my routines. I organized my home as it fits who I am and how it best works for my life. Bit by bit I worked through my pain and created a life with meaningful relationships and purposeful tasks. It is a life with joy. I laugh with friends over dinner. I get up in the morning eager to engage the new day. I make my cup of coffee and look out the back window . . . though my heart sinks at that gorgeous sight in the springtime without the sound of her voice exclaiming over the sheer beauty of a yard ablaze in white and pink.

I am buoyed by the fulfillment and meaning in my life. The windows of grief are much narrower than before, though in the moment the pain is so familiar. Familiar, yet different. As I pour out my tears now—my scattered showers—I remain in touch with the grounding of my present-tense reality of a new and good life that is before me.

I began the transition earlier with feeling "less bad," with a reluctant acceptance of my new reality. Then I began to feel pretty good. I was doing the things I enjoyed and found meaningful—writing, reading, spending time with family and friends.

Increasingly, when I thought of Karen it was with a smile, with such fondness, gratitude, and joy. A friend and mentor told me long ago that one can tell they are healing from a loss when they think of their loved one and "they first think, not of their death, but of their life." Often now, I find that I first think of her life, and I smile.

A Knock at the Door

Late one Saturday night Karen and I were still up watching television. There was a sharp knock at the door. It startled us. When I opened the door, two county police officers stood in front of me. "Are you Ron Greer?" one of them asked.

"Yes," I said. "Can I help you?"

Gesturing across the street, the police officer's voice lowered. "Your neighbors asked us to see if you could come over for a bit. Their daughter died this afternoon."

I got my coat and went immediately. I knew that the neighbors didn't seek me out because I was a counselor or pastor. They knew that Karen and I had lost a child, and that we—unlike almost anyone else—might understand what they were facing. They wanted someone who could "get it."

Today, you, the reader, and I get it. Our spouses have died. We have faced the raw grief of that loss. We know what it is like. We get it.

Be prepared for knocks at your door. Be prepared to reach down into that dark space and offer a lift of compassion, support, empathy, and presence. You know what you needed, and one day it may be yours to offer.

The knock at the door is certain to come. You get it, and you will give.

Stronger for
Having Been There

We don't come back as the same people who go into this heartache. Tragically, some don't come back at all. Some spirits are permanently broken by the experience. They never rebound following their loss. We can see it in their bitterness, their depression, in their lives without hope. Each person is unique, of course, but many didn't know how to mourn or lacked the courage or, perhaps, the vision of the hope that is to be found by engaging the process.

That must not be us.

We are victims of our spouses' deaths—but we must not remain there. Victim must not become our identity. It is something that happened to us; it is not who we are. We can persevere through our grief and rebound with resiliency. Resiliency is the capacity to recover from difficulties, to come back from an ordeal. And how do we come back? We can come back the stronger for having been there.

We can build on that resiliency, instead of living in vulnerability. With new clarity, we can gain a greater depth and wisdom, more meaningful relationships, and a better focus on what truly matters. We will have grown.

The growth comes from having reached down and drawn on strengths within that we never knew we had. We then claim those strengths as a part of who we are as we move forward with a new awareness and confidence. This may well include those who begin this struggle traumatized yet engaging their challenges with resilience.

I think of the countless persons to whom I have listened over these many years, as they have shared the stories of their lives. Of how they have responded to challenges. Of how they have dealt with struggles, even heartbreaking incidents. Often, I have found myself listening with awe at the personal strength they discovered and from which they drew in meeting that trial. Something within them knew the capacity was there, to be discovered. And they did. With insight. With courage. Yes, with resilience.

The experience of those who do engage their grief, who do muster the courage to endure the pain, who see this journey as a struggle laced with hope—well, you can see it in their countenance. After time has passed, there is a clarity, a confidence, a wisdom from one who has been there—a wisdom of one who knows. It is the wisdom of one who has been at life's center and has returned with an assurance of what matters, a confidence of knowing who they are and of what they are made, and a wisdom of having experienced moments of emotion more deeply and intimately than ever before.

As we rebuild our lives, the lowest places may well become our foundation—a remarkably solid foundation. We have learned from having to go where we never wished to go and forced to draw on strengths we did not previously know we had. So, we can well emerge from this nightmare the stronger for having been there.

Intentional

As I was busy with something one morning, I was distracted by the music playing in the background. I recognized a mournful Michael Bolton song, "How Am I Supposed to Live Without You?" and immediately I was undone.

Well, so much for whatever I had been doing.

Just how am I supposed to live without her? So much of me was wrapped up in being with her. It is a new day and now time to reset my sails and find new purposes and sources of meaning for my life—as I always embrace the memory of this precious lady. My life would go on. It would be decidedly different, but I would be intentional about making it the best it could be.

Yes, intentional. We have been intentional on this journey—looking squarely into the face of our loss and consciously mourning our hearts out. As we begin this new chapter, it is time to be just as intentional in carving out our new lives—as lives we will enjoy and value. We don't drift into living purposefully. Perhaps that is why it's called "doing it on purpose." How will we define this coming phase of our lives?

I am affected by what happens to me, but it is up to me to play it well, whatever hand I am dealt. How I play it will be integral in setting the tone for the rest of my life. I hope to do it deliberately and do it well.

If I were looking at my current life—my family, my friendships, a work that is meaningful and fulfilling, a faith that sustains—I would call it absolutely blessed. It is diminished only as I look through the eyes of grief, of whom I lost. Yet I have so much still, so much to work with as I move forward.

Those who emotionally grow through their mourning are the ones who engage their grief openly and fully, who feel the depth of it all, and who have the wisdom to learn of the strength they have discovered from within. From their time in the valley, they now see with new light, as never before, of what they are made. As never before, they go forward knowing all they bring to each of life's challenges. Yes, with a new confidence they go forward into the next chapter.

As time has passed, it has become clear that I have more with which to work than I had realized. As I have mourned, I have healed. As I have healed, I have grown. I will continue to emerge from the valley of grief with a clarity and life awareness as never before. In each of our moments of heartache, a special grace is there as we grow in maturity, insight, and confidence. Perhaps the pain of our grief is the tuition we pay for the education of all the life lessons gained and strengths realized.

Not Yet

"For everything there is a season and a time for every matter under heaven," begins that familiar passage from Ecclesiastes (3:1). I wondered, to what purpose is this season of my life—and of yours? With the mammoth task of grief dominating our attention, there has been no time or inclination to focus on such things. Now, perhaps, we have just enough bandwidth available to look beyond our heartaches to what may be coming.

So, here we are. We didn't choose to be here or want to be here. But this is where we are. We had no voice in how our lives would be so radically changed, but we do have a say in the shape and quality of where these changed lives will go from here. How shall we each begin?

To what do we feel inclined, or even called? This may be a time to look at options and opportunities to which we can offer our abilities, interests, time, and energy. It may be purely for enjoyment, to finally savor some of those moments again, or to connect with those who matter to us, to have some fun for a change. What's next may be to discern ways to make a difference, to enrich our communities, or to reach out to others who may also be struggling. Perhaps you simply may want to read a book, take a class, delve into a topic on which you have always had an interest but never the time. Or, and this really sounds appealing to those of us of a certain age, relish more time with grandkids!

For what purpose is this your season?

Listen for your voice—your own voice as it discerns what is the avenue for you to take at this distinct moment of your life. You have never been here before. Neither had I. As I turned the page and began this new season of my life, what you are reading just now is the result. I discovered I wanted to write about where I had been and what I had been through. I wanted to use that experience in a way that might matter to those who suffer the loss of their husband or wife. Something that might make a difference.

For what purpose is this your season, from which your life will find meaning and fulfillment and even joy?

Years ago, Karen and I were visiting the city of Savannah, Georgia. As we were walking through the beautiful garden squares of that historic city, we had a question about one of the sites. A sharply dressed older man with his bow tie and sport coat was walking toward us. He seemed clearly to be a local resident, which he confirmed he was. He was delightful. We talked about Savannah and its rich history. At some point, I asked him, "Have you lived here all your life?" I shall never forget his response. "Not yet."

It's the same for us. We have more life stretching out before us. It is not the life we wished for. But it is the one we have, and we can make it a good one. How will we choose to live it?

Grief After Grief

Much that we do in this time of mourning is based on one single and vital criterion. We do it when the time is right for us. Not before. Not later.

Wait until the time is right for you. Of all the choices for which timing is optional, don't put away, give away, or throw away anything of your spouse's until your heart says the time is right for you to do so. Neither rush nor delay. I believe, without pushing or pressing yourself to do anything, you will increasingly discover when the time is right for you. Honor that voice.

When we lose a husband or a wife, we likely are parting with someone with whom we have lived for years, decades. There is a home filled with belongings that were theirs. A home filled with reminders of their lives and our connection with them. As it was heartbreaking to say goodbye to our partners, it is arduous to part with each reminder of them.

After some initial straightening up of the house in the weeks following Karen's death, I left things largely as they were. Every now and then I would put something away or discard an item that will never be used, but there was always a reluctance.

Why? Why the hesitation? Every change, every single change, no matter how small it may seem symbolizes that I am further away from when I was with her. Having her things around brings the comfort of the reminder of when she was here. Perhaps it subconsciously creates the illusion that she will be returning.

I know that as I mourn successfully, I will gain clarity that she is here in spirit and in memory. As I do, having her things around, those reminders, will no longer be quite as powerful. At least my brain kept telling my heart that. But, oh my, that can be slow in coming. Early on, as I would make any changes to her things, certainly to discard them, I would feel both a pain of grief and a twinge of a first cousin to guilt. The source of the grief was obvious. I would not be doing this had she not died. I was saying goodbye time after time, item after item, garment after garment. Everything I touched was something she would never use again, each blouse or pair of pants she would never wear. Grief after grief.

Then there was that twinge. That sense of guilt, though I knew I was guilty of nothing. These were her things I was moving around, about to give away or even throw away. It was a feeling of betrayal in moving what was hers, for the first time, without her blessing. Because she died.

The Lesson

One evening I was walking past the laundry room. As she was putting clothes into the machine, Karen looked over her shoulder at me and said, "Let me show you how to do this." That's all she said before she began with the washing tutorial. "Let me show you how to do this," without adding why I would soon need to know. She didn't say, and I didn't ask. We both knew.

A month later, she was gone.

She passed the baton to me in several ways, preparing me for what lay ahead. She was my loving partner as we shared our lives, and she was my loving partner as she said goodbye. In the gentlest, kindest ways, she prepared me for my life without her.

Recalibrating

Karen's service was on a Friday. The following morning, I was up early after a less-than-restful night's sleep and went for a long walk. As I was almost home, I saw a man I had never seen before walking his dog. With earbuds in his ears, he smiled the biggest smile, held up his tumbler of coffee and said, "A dog, a podcast, and coffee. Life could not be better."

I wished him a good day. Two thoughts hit me almost simultaneously. On hearing, "Life could not be better," my first was, "Actually, it could be a whole lot better. A whole lot better." My second thought was: Karen did not have a dog, didn't listen to podcasts, and didn't care for coffee—but, my word, he embodied her spirit of joy. And he reminded me that, one day, I hope to as well.

Months, then years, have now passed since that Saturday morning. I am pleased to report that my life has gotten "a whole lot better" than it was on that heartbroken day. As I have been mourning, I have been recalibrating. I have purposefully attended to how I can have the best life I possibly can have though, now, without Karen. I have been dealt a new hand. How do I best play this one? Purposefully, deliberately.

I have been recalibrating. I have done it many times in minor ways throughout my life, as have we all. I have known far lesser losses that required adjusting to new circumstances. I have moved forward, for instance, without the abilities that came with youth. I remember when I could no longer run marathons…and, later, when I could no longer run. I had always loved running. But no longer was that possible. It was disappointing. But I recalibrated. Now I walk instead. I have several paths I love to take as I enjoy the beauty of my hometown.

Karen has died. I no longer have the joy of her physical presence, though I relish how her spirit goes with me. I am recalibrating to a new life. I am happy most mornings as I experience life from a different place, from this new vantage point. My sense of well-being comes from this new foundation. As they say, I have reset my default position.

I cannot join the gentleman in saying, "Life could not be better." It certainly could. But this morning, I am happy.

39 Degrees

I had not been ready to give away Karen's clothes. As I have counseled countless clients, there is no prescribed time for this. The heart is the only authority on this subject that matters.

But it was January, and the high that day was to be 39 degrees. There were women throughout our city who were cold. They didn't have warm coats to wait for the bus to take them to work. Karen's coats hung in the foyer closets. They needed to get to women who deserved to be warm on a winter day. Karen would have liked that. She would have liked that a lot.

"39 degrees" was all I needed to read to know that the right time was now.

Two dear friends head our church's Restoration Partners Prison Ministry that facilitates the successful return to society of women who have been incarcerated. On the day of their release, this ministry gives them suitcases with clothes and toiletries. Otherwise, many of these women would be returning to the outside world with literally nothing. This would give them something. Something in which they would look good and feel proud and stay warm.

114

What it gave me was meaning. The idea of her coats going to this ministry had infused purpose into the gift. I was not just focused on where these coats *had been*. I now saw where they *were going*. It transformed the experience. It felt less like I was giving up a tangible reminder of Karen and far more like giving a part of Karen to someone who dearly needed it.

Our Rings

I took my wedding ring off on a Saturday in January. It was time. Karen had died almost five months before. I had been sensing it was time, but there was always that hesitation. In some way it felt like making what I know is real, even more real. It also felt like that familiar betrayal again. It was as if the choice to remove my ring from the finger on which she had placed it on our wedding day and where it has resided all these years, was disavowing my bride and my vows. I know it is illogical, but such is the way of the human heart.

It was time. The world in which I now lived was not the one of which my Karen was ever a part. Time had passed. A page had been turned with the passing of the months, and then the holidays ushered in a new year. She never lived in this year. How do I say this? For weeks, even months, this was her world, but she was missing from it. I kept expecting her voice to be calling from down the hall. I didn't any longer. Time has ushered me into a life I was creating without her. I either move forward or cease meaningfully to live. I was wearing a ring from the former world. It no longer fit where and who I am now.

It was time. Slipping it off was easier than I had expected. The time being right, of course, was why. So was the matter of where it was going. Karen's engagement ring was placed in a soft, cloth envelope just after she died. I took my ring off my finger, placed it beside hers, and gently folded the envelope closed. Metaphorically, it no longer fit on my finger. It fit perfectly in the cloth envelope, with hers, where it belonged.

I had always hoped I would know when it was time. I did. Her spirit would always be with me, but, in this world, my marriage to my Karen had ended with her death. It was time.

117

Karen's Clothes

Finally, it was time to give away nearly everything else.

Daily, as I got dressed, I would see Karen's side of the closet. It was still filled with all of her beautiful clothes. They had not been worn, or even touched, in all those months. Karen's blouses—especially her signature white blouses—and her pants and her outfits are simply beautiful. She had taste and a sense of style. These women coming out of prison, recipients of the church's ministry to support them in transition, could return to the world with dignity and pride—and one of them in that white blouse with the pleats down the front. If these outfits could no longer be Karen's, they should be theirs. It's what she would have chosen in a heartbeat. It was time to get them to the cleaners.

A clothes closet was set up at church for the returning citizens. A room was filled with women's clothes from which they would select the attire in which they would courageously step into the rest of their lives. With all the anxieties and insecurities they carry with them, it would help—a lot—if they felt good about how they looked.

At last, the day came as those from this ministry shopped, at no cost, for their new outfits. It would be with dignity, heads held high—dressed attractively in clothes donated by church members—that they would find their way into restored lives and selves.

All of Karen's clothes were there. My daughter Brooke and I were thoughtfully included in this big day in order to see these selections being made. It was an honor to see the excitement on the faces of these women as they chose some of Karen's outfits. Karen would have been so pleased to see her blouses, dresses, and pants going to those who needed them and were so enthusiastic to have them.

During the middle of the morning, one of our guests had a question. "Where are the price tags?" she asked. It was pure joy to watch her face immediately glow when she heard the words, "There are no price tags." Her smile was one of both delight and relief. I happened to see her later as our volunteers carefully placed the three garments she had chosen into a bag with pink tissue. Two of her selections had been Karen's. It was a moment to savor in knowing that her blouses were going to be used by someone who needed them and likely could not have purchased them.

Brooke said later that the day was not as difficult as she had expected—that her mom's clothes were no longer hers. They now belonged to those who need them. So wise and so true.

The Pendulum Swing

After the shopping event where Karen's clothes were distributed to women emerging from prison, I was seated at the table next to one of the guests who was clearly pleased with her selections. She was delightful. We talked and laughed as we ate. Then, for some reason, I glanced down at the floor. Between us, on the floor, she had placed her bag with the clothes she had just chosen. Our volunteers had folded her selections, neatly tucking them away in this large bag, then topping it off with the pink tissue billowing up on top. But the weight of the garments had shifted, tilting the tissue slightly to the side. Peeking out from beneath it was a most familiar black and white jacket. It had been Karen's. On seeing it, my emotional pendulum released and swung to the other side, to my other world.

Lunch soon concluded, and a photo was taken of the group. I said my goodbyes and got in my car. The tears came immediately and would not stop.

Watching with joy the returning citizens shop—and then mourning in grief all afternoon is a metaphor of what my life was like. The whole morning was one of gratitude—seeing her things go where they needed to go. I will always be thankful for this ministry providing the opportunity to connect her things with these women. But at lunch, my morning went to mourning.

I love the way a good friend put it. Her mother had lived a fulfilled and completed life. Soon after her mom died, she said, "So, each of my tears contain both sadness and joy."

This is my life. It is filled with blessings. I am fulfilled in countless ways. And Karen is gone. There is grief and emptiness in the midst of the joy. The joys of my current life and of my memories, the sadness of her death and of her absence. Both emotions are real. Both are held at the same time. The joy does not diminish the sadness. Nor does the sadness dilute the joy.

They are my two worlds, with two clusters of emotions, sitting side by side. Each felt deeply. They are parallel paths. Something about her clothes going into the closets of others—though I very much wanted that to happen—made the finality of her life again more vivid. Life had gone on. Now even her things had gone on: to good homes, to those who need them and will value them, to where I wanted them, and even more importantly, to where Karen would have wanted them to go. All of that is good. It is as it should be. It's just that it all, yet again, reminds me that she is gone, and, despite my longing, will not be coming back.

The closets are now empty. They are a tangible, visible moving away from the life that was, to the one that is to come.

Ron's Ron

A caring friend wrote me a kind and thoughtful note after Karen died. She expressed her hope that I was receiving plenty of support during these days. Then, acknowledging my counseling profession, she said the one thing she had been wondering was, "Who does Ron talk to? Who is Ron's Ron?"

I am surrounded by them. And they have made all the difference. Karen died at the end of the summer of 2020. COVID-19 was raging, and we were months away from a vaccine being available. So, I joined with friends, one at a time, for lunch on my outdoor patio. They would bring sandwiches, wanting to catch up and to hear how I was doing. Every morning for months, one friend would text me a song he thought I would enjoy. Another would send me photos of sunrises. With others, I would take walks. Each was Ron's Ron.

The work of grief is a task we largely engage within, each on our own. Oh, but the difference it makes in being surrounded by loving support! It buoys us. It renews us. It gives us energy for the task of mourning we must then reengage. These relationships mean the world.

There are among those friends ones to whom we can pour out our hearts. We can put it all out there, knowing we will be heard, and it will be held compassionately. With them, we give our pain a voice straight from the heart. And, in the expressing of it, a bit more of our grief is healed, and we are blessed.

Lifelines

Since we were each in our COVID-19 bubbles during the early months of my mourning Karen's death, I gained a perspective on loving support I would not have otherwise. There could be no hugs, no handshakes with the squeezing of the arm, no face-to-face expressions of care and concern without a mask or plenty of distance. Much personal intimacy had to be sacrificed for the greater good of physical health. Something is diminished when empathy is muffled by a mask and voices are projected from a safe distance away. Medically, so much was gained with these precautions. Emotionally, so much was lost.

Yet, what I came to discover is that caring doesn't require hugs—only genuinely compassionate hearts desiring to express their love. It made a profound difference as countless friends and acquaintances reached out with cards or emails or texts or calls or an invitation to that across-the-porch cup of coffee. In the COVID-19 era, these were the means by which we expressed our love, the vehicles by which we delivered our compassion to those who needed it most.

I confess. I had always thought of a sympathy card as being a polite, formal gesture of condolence. Well intended. Well done. But rather lightweight. I was wrong.

I have a long, steep driveway to walk back from the mailbox each afternoon. For those of you who send cards to the bereaved, please know there were days I was in tears before I got back up to the house. I had not yet read the card. I had not even opened it. Yet my heart was already touched, and exceedingly appreciative, that someone cared enough to write.

Back at the kitchen table I opened it. They wrote to me of Karen and the exemplary life she lived. They wrote to me of their love and support during that difficult time. More tears came. They needed to. To express my grief, through tears or words, was the only way to get through the valley. To give it a voice. They may have thought they were just sending me a card. No. They sent me a lifeline. They sent me a means to do the work, to engage the task of mourning I needed to engage. They facilitated connecting me with my tenderness as they embraced me with their support.

A Gift of Grace

Compassion is offered in many forms. Each expression is true to the personality of the one offering their care. By each our souls are fed and our hearts are touched. By each we are nourished and readied for the next leg of the journey.

I have a friend who called me three weeks after Karen died asking if I was doing anything Thursday afternoon. Not a thing. Good, then "meet us in front of our building at 4:30." I did, and she and her husband took me to the grocery store. There she walked me through every section of the grocery store, attentively coaching me on what to look for and what to get. I shall always remember learning the nuances in selecting the finest brussels sprouts.

As dear friends, they were keenly aware how little I knew of my way around the grocery store. As she was escorting me through this new experience, she was introducing me to this era of the life journey I had now entered.

Then they took me back to their condo where the lessons began. With each dish she prepared she handed me a recipe card she had written out in advance. I watched and learned how, step by step, to bake salmon and roast vegetables—which I have done countless times since. My grief was still fresh as I sat with them at their dining table.

We ate, we reflected, and we remembered. This was a gift of grace that nourished me in more ways than one.

The Gift of Presence

Presence is to give full attention to the one before us.

We can feel it. They are with us. They are for us. By the grace of their presence, we know we are not alone. They are by our side and nowhere else. Nothing else matters. We talk. We sit silently. Whatever fits the moment. We are together.

Presence is not active. Presence is a state of being.

Grief is a terribly lonely experience—we all need the company of those who truly care. For some, their presence is softly spoken, even quiet. They will stop by and sit for a time, unhurried, to catch up on how we are doing. They bring a warm presence. They know we each need someone caring enough to visit, courageous enough to ask how we are feeling, and wise enough to be quiet and listen.

Those moments can be sacramental. Their compassion can be transforming.

If something profound is spoken, that is not what touches those of us who are grieving. It's not *what* we hear, it's that we *are heard*.

That caring presence comes from the heart, but it's seen in the eyes. What shows is that someone has come to join us, truly to be with us.

Those moments together may define empathy, yet, let me define it in one other way. The root word for empathy comes from the Latin *pathos*, meaning suffering. The "em" means "in." In suffering. Empathy is to be in it: in the moment, in the relationship, in the presence of the one who is suffering.

They open their hearts to be fully in the moment as we share our grief. They are engaged. Personally, compassionately with us. It takes presence to a new depth that includes resonance.

No one can feel the emotions of another. Each of our hearts walks its own path. Yet, with empathy, a friend allows their heart to be touched by our suffering. And we know we are not alone. Not only are they with us—in that they showed up—but they resonate with what we are going through.

They have allowed themselves to access that place in their hearts that parallels the pain in ours. Their hearts align with ours. With courage and caring, they get it. That's what we see in their eyes. That's what we feel from their hearts. We are touched by the closeness, the intimacy of their compassion, and we do not feel so alone on our journey.

In whatever way they share their compassion with you as you mourn, let them in. Let them love you. I don't care that you are the one who is always giving and caring and doing. Not now. Not this time. Let them love you. They came to be with you. And it will mean the world to you.

Open your heart to those you love and trust. With those we love and trust, we can talk it out. They bring to us the precious gifts of wanting to know and of wanting to offer us the opportunity to talk it through. Share with them the feelings of your heart. Not all tears have to be liquid. Some can be formed in words.

I am often asked by those who want to express their loving kindness to someone who is mourning, "What do I say?" I always respond that it doesn't matter what you say nearly so much as who you are with them. Your presence, your caring, your compassion will speak far more eloquently than any words.

We don't remember the words. We only remember, and cherish, their presence. There can be the longest line circling the Fellowship Hall following a memorial service. Countless friends waiting to speak to the bereaved. And this grieving wife will recall not a single word anyone spoke to her. However, she will always remember and be strengthened by their faces and their embraces.

It's their presence. They showed up. It's not what they said; it's that they were there.

Then, having expressed this as clearly as I know how, they will respond, "Yeah, I know you're right. But still, what do I say?"

"Okay," I respond. "You say your version of these three caring affirmations: 'I love you.' 'I am so sorry you are having to go through this.' 'I am here for you.'" You are offering three things: Your love. Your empathy. Your support. Those are the gifts you bring. Put them into words if you like, but those are the messages your presence already brought.

In that time of grief, we need our community.

We need them to be open, loving, and listening.

We need them to be themselves.

We need them to engage, not back away.

We need compassion, not cliches.

We need presence, not platitudes.

And we need them to speak our spouse's name.

It Is Well with My Soul

A pastor friend sent me a text with a single line, asking simply, "How is it with your soul, my friend?" The question gave me the opportunity to pause and reflect. My response was, "My heart is heavy, but it is well with my soul." Consistently, I felt the spiritual presence and grace of the Divine with me. And I had the additional advantage of having God's many messengers bringing that love in countless ways.

Spiritual writers refer to the importance of accessing our true or authentic selves. To live out of that dimension of who we are is to live genuinely, spiritually. One's true self is distinguished from the developed identity we invent as we learn who we are supposed to be from our culture and upbringing. That is our constructed identity. Our true selves are the authentic persons beneath the created exterior. It is to my *true self* I go in my mourning. Emotionally, spiritually I am taken all the way to the ground floor.

Hope in the Night

My mourning for the past months has had many dimensions, and one important one is an intense spiritual experience. My times of personal emotion have taken me to a level within my heart and soul I visit too rarely. While the pain, the absolute ache to have Karen back has been horrific, with each wave of grief washing over me I have been connected—in the midst of the grief itself—with a depth I can only call my soul. And at that foundation I am in the presence of what I know as God.

What comes to mind as a parallel to my experience is that passage from Matthew (6:6) where Jesus speaks about achieving profound, spiritual moments, "But whenever you pray, go into your room and shut the door." My grieving is just such a spiritual moment. My emotions have taken me into my room, my mourning has closed the door, and I have raw access to the authentic person God created in me—and there I feel the spirit of the Divine.

I think of the verse from the Beatitudes, "Blessed are those who mourn, for they will be comforted" (Matthew 5:4). Or as another translation phrases the second half of that verse,

"Only then can you be embraced by the One most dear to you" (Matthew 5:4, MSG). Yes, mourning can be an embrace, or perhaps an invitation to a new spiritual awareness.

We all look forward to the sun breaking through at the far end of this valley as the wound moves toward healing. But maybe instead of always looking past my grief—for when I get *through* the valley as my time of flourishing—perhaps, just perhaps, it is also *in* this time of pain and not just beyond it. There is insight, self-awareness, growth that can be gained only from the effort, and sometimes the wounds, of life's struggles. Through the ordeal, we become enlightened and strengthened.

Through this whole experience of grief, I am being continually transformed. As with the heartbreaking death of our son decades ago, I have been pushed to a depth I have rarely accessed in the years between these two losses. Make no mistake, I don't want to live in the pain of that emotional level. I couldn't take it. But I value and have grown from the meaningful, difficult visits there.

God can help us use, to our advantage, any hand life deals us.

Within every darkness, there is grace. That grace—the gifts we gain from the darkness of the night—often include resiliency, character, and wisdom.

I think of times of struggle or grief or distress in my life as visits to a place within I can only call my soul. I go there, as do you, and return *changed*, having grown.

Yes, we are blessed *from* the very darkness with which we struggled and suffered.

If your loss is recent, I know this may well sound like insanity. For you, it is far too early for this to be conceivable, much less yet possible. Continue with your mourning. A new day will come, but it can't be hurried.

We all love to live in the light where we know laughter and joy. Goodness knows, I do. But it is usually in the darkness that we develop and deepen and mature. My most meaningful growth has come out of the darkness of my grief, my failures, and my struggles.

Some lights can be seen, some grace can be known only from the darkness. Remember how the wise men were guided by the light? They followed a star—a light they could see only in the darkness.

Though the times of darkness are painful and distressing, the light, the hope is there. And often we don't have to wait for the day to begin to experience the illumination, the wisdom of the night.

This is what Paul meant when he wrote, "Suffering produces endurance, and endurance produces character, and character produces hope, and hope does not disappoint us" (Romans 5:3b-5).

Paul's insight is important in our grief journey. If we will engage the suffering of our mourning, consistently, with endurance—staying with it as each wave comes over us—then a new strength of character within us will begin to develop. The origin of the word character meant "to engrave" or "to cut into grooves." The courage to mourn with endurance, to engage whatever life brings, engraves the wisdom and maturity onto our hearts. As that new grounding emerges, it offers us confidence. It is a confidence in who we are and confidence in a life ahead. It is a confidence we call hope.

This is the hope of the night.

Hope in the Light

There is another hope for those of us who are mourning: the hope of the new day. There is a passage from the Psalms that speaks to this hope with which persons of faith live in these times: "Weeping may linger for the night, but joy comes with the morning" (30:5). We are a people of hope.

Hope that our husbands and wives are in gracious, eternal care.

Hope that grace and support will be with us through this time.

Hope that we will come out of this ordeal the stronger for having been there.

Hope that our relationships with those we lost will continue in rich and meaningful ways, in our memories and in our hearts.

Hope that we will carve out new lives—different, but good—for ourselves.

And hope that, as we heal, the day will break, and joy will come with the morning.

Following the death of someone so important to us, do we eventually return to the life we knew? Can we go back? Of course not. But we can go forward.

Can we be happy again? Yes.

Can we lead full lives again? Yes.

After such a loss, will we be free of the pain? No.

Will we tear up when a reminder sneaks up on us? Of course, we will. Those scattered showers are in the forecast.

A client came in for a counseling session some years after I had last seen her. I asked how she was doing. She said, "I'm doing really well. Now, I've still got my baggage, but at least I'm down to a carry-on."

After a profound personal loss, that may be our goal. To have worked through our grief so thoroughly that we are down to a carry-on.

Full, happy lives are what we can lead, after a time, following a loss. But after a big one like the loss of a spouse, no matter how much time passes, every so often there will be a hitch in the stride and a tear in the eye.

The Glory of Their Spirit

For much of the twentieth century it was believed that the goal of grieving was breaking the attachment with our loved ones who died, so we could move on and get over it.

I will *always* be attached to those I love. I will never fully get over the major loves and losses in my life. Nor do I want to, nor do I need to in order to live a full, meaningful, and joyful life. And now the professional world that studies grieving—the field of thanatology—knows that. In our mourning we are not breaking attachments—we are redefining *how* we are attached.

Though I have said goodbye to my wife, my love for her and my feeling of connection with her live on. This is not denial. I am fully and painfully aware that she has died. Yet, I am fully and joyfully aware of the ways I am connected that continue still.

Every day I was away from those I loved. I said goodbye in the morning and was not back home until that evening. But though I was away for hours, or even days at a time, I still loved them and felt a close, personal connection while we were apart. Now, though I said goodbye to Karen, I still love her and feel a close, personal connection though we are apart. From her life I will always be inspired and enriched.

Death does not end that. Death does not end that connection. For fifty years I loved my wife. I've loved her every day since. Just as I valued—savored—loving her in her presence, I value and savor loving her in her absence as I remember. For in my heart, she will always have her place.

On the walls of the chapel at the American Cemetery in Normandy, France, chiseled in white limestone, are these words:

"Think not only upon their passing,
remember the glory of their spirit."

We do think often of their passing, and we mourn deeply. Yet we shall remember and honor and be inspired by the glory of their spirit.

We have all said our goodbyes—yet, thank God, those we love and have lost go with us still.

The Quiet House

A sacred moment happened at bedtime on the evening before Karen died. She was not able to speak on the last day of her life beyond a faint whisper of "yes" or "no," and was barely audible the day before. On that evening—the day before—fatigued, exhausted, we got her to bed very early. I tucked her in and talked with her briefly, but she was able to say nothing. Her eyes were closed. She was now asleep. I kissed her goodnight and began leaving the room.

I had reached the foot of the bed, and to my astonishment she lifted her head off the pillow. The effort it took, with so little strength left, is beyond description. Her eyes locked intently onto mine, and, slowly, intentionally forming each word, she offered me her final gift, "Ron...I...love...you."

When the house became quiet the first time there was a jolting awareness that Karen had actually died. She was gone. When she had been with me there was motion, activity. There was the sound of her voice as she called to me, the squeak of the floor upstairs as she walked above me, the familiar noises of the kitchen as dinner was being prepared. The sounds of her presence.

Then she was gone. On that Thanksgiving afternoon—the first without her—I walked back from waving goodbye to my family into a house void of the sound of the relationship I had known and adored for fifty years. Quiet. Simply the absence of sound brought on such a deep ache. Not surprisingly, as I settled into my new life, I just happened to buy new speakers for my sound system. They were placed all around. It had gotten way too quiet around here.

Ironically, *quiet* had always had such a positive connotation for me. I have one of those minds that is always in motion, internally chattering away. Always thinking of what to do now, then what to do next. I think of the cartoon I saw of a couple sitting under an umbrella on the beach. It was indeed Karen and me. You can tell what the husband had just said as the wife responds, "We *are* doing something. You're just not very good at it." That was us.

So, for me, quiet was always a blessed reprieve. It was refreshing, relaxing, restoring. I would meditate to achieve quiet, peace. Arriving at a soulful place. But following Karen's death, quiet was a reminder of her absence and my loss. Instead of solitude, it brought loneliness.

Then time passed. Much grief was felt. Many tears were shed. And healing began. Genuine, substantive healing began slowly and continued steadily. And now, as I write this, I continue through the valley, but I'm much further along. As grief is less dominant in my heart, *quiet* is reclaiming its place of peace. My spirit can again arrive at that soulful depth and be restored.

In the quiet, I meditate again, opening my soul to the presence of God.

In the quiet, I continue to be reminded of Karen, but now, of how her spirit goes with me. Though I miss her physical presence, I am buoyed and enriched and forever grateful.

My peace I leave with you.

9 781791 028800